DANUBE

DAN

UBE

Irina Georgescu

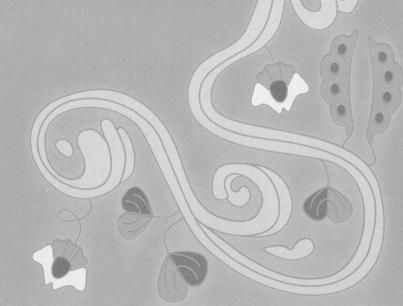

Hardie Grant

BOOKS

Chapter One

FIRST STEPS ON EASTERN LANDS

•••

Chapter Two

A LAND OF MILLERS

•••

Chapter Three

A LAND TO SHARE

•••

Chapter Four

A LAND OF BROTHS

•••

Introduction

This is a book about the lands of the river Danube meandering eastwards between Romania, Serbia and Bulgaria.

With every page you turn, you will visit new places, meet new people and discover how they eat at home. The recipes are simple, comforting and reasonable in all seasons. A lot of them are vegetarian, some with meat, and only a few with fish, but for me – and I hope for you too – the book is more than this. It is about the stories and the anecdotes, the glimpses into the past and the celebration of local flavours.

My ancestral home, Romania, has a complex history and an eclectic ethnic fabric that reflects the tumultuous past of these Eastern river lands. Here, the Danube forms most of its lower basin, turning into a beautiful delta, a UNESCO site, before it joins the Black Sea.

We start our culinary quest in the Banat region, follow the river south into the historic Walachia and finish east in Dobrogea. We'll explore Serbian and Bulgarian culinary traditions in these borderlands, and more, since these are some of Eastern Europe's most ethnically diverse regions.

We will discover how people eat at home.

The cuisine in Romania is a blend of Central European and Balkan influences, hence we use staple ingredients that are also easily accessible outside the country. The way we cook at home is more varied and regional than what you can see in restaurants, which often serve a standard menu across the country. We have old traditions of preserving and cooking with seasonal fruit and vegetables, influenced by observing 180 days of Lent (luckily not in a row). I never starve on Lent days because I can choose from various salads, dips and spreads, refreshing broths with vegetables, and slow-cooked beans and pulses enhanced by the combination of sweet and sour flavours. These dishes are never boring, and I like to serve grilled flatbreads with them or soak dollops of golden polenta or spoonfuls of noodles in their rich sauces. Even when we cook with meat or fish, the recipes use spring onions (scallions), leeks, chard, spinach, courgettes (zucchini), aubergines (eggplants) and tomatoes. You won't believe the variety.

The landscape in Romania has allowed for a cuisine of plenty.

The Carpathian mountains gave us the pastoral traditions you can see in the different types of cheeses we make: the curd cheese, soft and good in fillings and toppings; the *caș* with its flavour of fresh milk; the *telemea*, the hard, brined cheese that we serve as a starter with fruit brandy; the *burduf* cheese and *cașcaval*, with their mild spiciness good for melting. This cheesemaking is not something we learned or took from other cultures; it is a way of life influenced by the mountains.

The soft hills and vast plains in the south, nourished by many rivers that flow into the Danube, are perfect for growing wheat, including barley, burghul and maize. It's a miller's land, producing the high-quality flour needed for filo pastry, to be used in numerous pies, and for noodles. It's also a vegetable grower's land, from small gardens at the back of every house to large areas dedicated to greens, leaves and legumes. The rivers give us freshwater fish, the carp and trout we are so fond of and cook with so much pleasure. Meat is mostly pork and beef, lamb is considered seasonal and only for Easter, while the mutton goes into sausages and pastrami.

It's a diverse cuisine, whose main ingredient is generosity.

My grandfather, Gheorghe, was from the South, from a region called Oltenia. Here people are renowned for their short temper and resilience, even stubbornness, but also for their generosity. When he opened the door to his house, he opened the door to his heart, and the way to express this love was by giving us a lot to eat, plus seconds and more to take home. 'Bring more, the girls are still hungry,' he used to say to my grandmother Domnica after we all had eaten at least a round of everything. The girls were my mother, aunties and my sister and I. His stories about the Oltenian ash bread captured my imagination since it was impossible to make in an apartment. How the embers were put around and on top of this clay cloche to bake the bread sounded like something from the mythology tales I used to read. My grandmother cooked from these stories, and together we stuffed peppers for soup that was red as crayfish, cooked leeks with olives, made dock leaf parcels to char on a flat iron and sprinkle with garlic. Like my grandfather, people in the South are impatient and want their food to be on the table quickly.

This is my mantra for the recipes: quick and bold,
just like the people along the Danube.

Historians think that this swiftness, reflected in how we live and speak in the South, especially in Oltenia, is down to the impetuous temperament of the ancient Romans. You will read in this book that it is here in the South that the Roman Empire emerged victorious after many unsuccessful clashes with the Dacians and Getae tribes. The victory was celebrated on a monument dedicated to these battles, Trajan's Column, which you can see today in Rome. Over the centuries, this lineage had given its name to the first independent principality near the Danube, the Romanian Principality, also known as Walachia, and later, the name of the country: Romania. Walachia comes from Vlach, a nickname given by German tribes to former colonies of the Roman Empire. This is also the root of another name: Wales, my home in the UK.

While testing the recipes in this book, I constantly found culinary clues from the Roman Empire: the leeks, so loved by the Romans, are the culinary symbol of Oltenia (and Wales); we still bake the ash bread under *testum*, earthenware pots,

like in Pompei; we add vinegar to soups, an old Roman ingredient, to which they were almost addicted; and lovage and parsley, that used to flavour many ancient Roman dishes. The similarities stop at garlic, which Romans hated, but we love and use in abundance.

A cuisine of many influences.

In one of my other books, *Tava*, I told the story of some of Romania's ethnic groups through their most important recipes. In *Danube*, I follow a similar path and take you to the homes of five more communities, where they will cook their family dishes. From the Slavic people of the Iron Gates to the Turkic people of Dobrogea, it is from their culinary ingenuity and wisdom that these local cuisines formed our national cuisine. I use 'national' here in the sense of what people eat across the country, the archetypal dishes, what people remember from their childhood and also what they don't remember. In Romania and its neighbours across the Danube, Bulgaria and Serbia, we need to skip around 60 years in our trip down the culinary memory lane, skip the Communist regime that made us forget how we used to eat. Discovering our past means saving and encouraging our regional and ethnic diversity and appreciating our comfort food.

If there is no cornmeal, there is no meal.

I often say that we eat cornmeal more than the Italians. It's true. Coming from the Americas, it was introduced to these lands by the Ottoman Empire, trading with the Venetian and Genoese merchants. Alex Drace-Francis, in his book *The Making of Mămăligă*, finds maize well established in the 1700s throughout the Carpathian and Danubian area. The plant's presence here was partly a product of these lands 'situation at the intersection of trade routes, partly a result of the dramatic encounters between the Habsburg and Ottoman land armies in these provinces [...].' It was indeed warfare that determined the intense cultivation of maize in centuries to come. These borderlands between Empires encouraged a maize market between landowners and armies. The fact that it could grow in the hills and mountains and give better, more reliable yields than wheat was a major advantage. Plus, it was cheaper and readily available. Cooking a cornmeal dish, *mămăligă*, to satisfy the soldiers' hunger took less fuel and was quicker than making bread. It became the crop to fall on if wheat wasn't enough for civilians, and the rescue plan for Princes to feed their people.

This is how *mămăligă* entered our homes across the country and became a glorious national dish. Throughout this book, you will discover its many stories and versions: simmered, baked or fried. We like to turn it onto a chopping board, allow it to cool, then use a string to cut neat slices.

This is the mother recipe, the one you will prepare throughout this book using store-bought polenta (cornmeal).

SEE OVERLEAF →

Mămăligă, Polenta

CORNMEAL

I make *mămăligă* often; it is a comfort food, and during the pandemic, I even ran cookery classes on how to cook with it. If you can find stone ground cornmeal with all the goodness of the whole grain in it, buy it and enjoy the true flavour of corn without the need to add anything else. Use it following the instructions on the packet. Otherwise, I buy it in regular shops and supermarkets, where you can find it as polenta. You need to choose the one where you can see its golden, finely crushed kernels and not the variety that looks like a pale yellow powder. Sometimes it's called medium ground, other times finely ground, but whatever the name, choose by colour and texture. In many shops, cornmeal is labelled as polenta. To avoid confusion, I use the term 'polenta (cornmeal)' throughout the book.

A good start for your *Mămăligă* Polenta is 1 part cornmeal to 4 parts liquid (water, milk or stock).

Serves 4

800 ml (27 fl oz/ 3⅓ cups) water
1 teaspoon salt
200 g (7 oz/ 1⅓ cups) polenta (cornmeal)
25 g (1 oz) salted butter

Bring the water with salt to the boil. Use a whisk to stir the cornmeal in, turn the heat to low, cover the pan and allow the water to be absorbed slowly. You don't need to stir continuously, only a couple of times, to help the cornmeal absorb the water evenly. When it's ready, turn off the heat, add the butter and keep the pan covered until you are ready to serve.

...and with this recipe, we are ready to begin. Let's go.

IRINA GEORGESCU

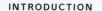

FIRST
STEPS
ON

EASTERN LANDS

The Iron Gates
and the Fig Trees
in Sviniţa Village

It is here that we start our journey along the lower Danube, in western Romania, where the river enters the country. The Iron Gates are a dramatic landscape of steep cliffs overlooking the river, which enclose the Danube Gorge between Romania and Serbia. 'Travelling through the Iron Gates, by road or boat, I have the sense of an umbilical cord. The river is very deep here – as deep as the ledges off the Black Sea coast at the Danube mouth. It is exhilarating to be trapped between cliffs, with so much water below and sky above,' wrote Nick Thorpe in his epic book, *Danube*. I felt the same when following the old riverside roads built by the Romans to bring the armies closer to defeating the Dacian tribes. As a traveller, you are in awe of the majestic sight that unfolds in front of you. Dacians were Romanians' ancestors; their defeat was celebrated on Emperor Trajan's Column, which can be seen today in Rome near the Colosseum. Trajan's military ambitions led to the construction of the longest bridge over a river in ancient Rome, just south of the Gorge, at Drobeta-Turnu Severin, where you can still see the foot of the bridge on the Romanian side.

The waters on this stretch are dotted with vestiges of structures, half-sunk or poking their heads out when the river level is low. They are not just Roman, but Slavic and Turkish too, like the Tricule (Three Towers), remnants of a 15th-century surveillance and defence structure. Old rocks stay put in the middle of the river, of which Babacaia is the most photographed of all. Giant chains used to stretch from two fortresses on opposite banks in Serbia and Romania, nailed into this rock and lifted to prevent ships from entering the gorge without paying the toll.

However, it is the land that tells a better story. One of the oldest Mesolithic settlements in Europe was discovered on the Serbian bank in 1960 at Lepensky Vir. Together with the artefacts found on the Romanian bank, they illuminate us about the 13,000-year-old culture that is now known as the Iron Gates Mesolithic. The mountains on the Romanian side form Banatul de Clisură, a region that from the Middle Ages to the 20th century had successively been in the possession of the Hungarians, the Ottomans, the Serbs and the Habsburgs. Now it is divided between Romania, Serbia and Hungary.

The Food is Ready, 'Invade, People!'

Romanians' shared history with the Serbs goes way back to the 6th century, when Slavic tribes migrated south towards the Balkans and later adopted the Christian religion. It is this religion that has strengthened the bond between Romanians and Serbs, basically two different peoples, one Latin and the other Slavic. When the Ottoman expansion put this religion in danger in a later century, the Serbs moved their diocese across the Danube, from Belgrade to Banat in Timișoara, Romania. They found refuge in these lands and also spread throughout the country, north and east.

When I started my journey along the Iron Gates road, past the Babacaia rock, I stopped at a local producer's hut laden with a variety of jam jars and small colourful bottles. 'It's fig jam from the Serbian villages on the slopes of these mountains,' said the seller pointing further down the road and up to the peaks. Here, the warm and humid climate trapped between the mountains is perfect for fig trees. 'And in these bottles, we have fig brandy,' which suddenly made sense in a country that loves a fruit brandy called *țuică*. Most importantly, the figs became a regional brand and a good pull for tourists every summer. So, the next day, I was delighted that my host Lina Dragotoiu and her daughter Radmila offered me coffee and fig jam for breakfast (see recipe on page 247). In Serbian, when the food is ready, you don't say *bon appetit*, but *navali narode*, which means 'invade, people!' It's exactly what I did that morning.

I stayed in the most iconic Serbian village in Romania called Svinița, up in the mountains with a jaw-dropping view of the Danube Gorge. A former teacher, Mrs Lina is now the president of the Svinicanke Women's Association in the village, which meets regularly to keep traditions alive and pass them down to the youngsters in the community.

Like many villages that struggled after the collapse of the mining industry triggered by the fall of the Communist regime in 1989, people turned to tourism for survival. Today, local produce, local guesthouses, local traditions and the famous Fig Festival bring hundreds of tourists here. This success is noticeable in the way Svinița is run: good roads, well-kept houses and a progressive vision for the future. What I sensed above all was the pride of being Serbian, something this ethnicity and nation have had since their ancient beginnings.

Praznic

One of the most important events in the life of the Serbian ethnic community is related to a religious event called Slava or Praznic, the Saint Protector of the House. It is a custom with roots in prehistory that was adopted by Orthodoxy, so Romanians also celebrate it as Hram. The saint is usually chosen on the day a couple gets married, whether from previous saints in the family or the closest saint to the wedding day. From this moment onwards, everything they do is under its protection: a new house, the birth of children, every new beginning or important moments in life. To give thanks, the saint is celebrated on the same day every year. In Mrs Lina's family, for instance, it is St. Nicolas in December, and the entire family comes together around the table.

Traditionally, the gatherings were organised over three days, bringing together the whole family and close friends. It started with a dinner, continued the next day with a lunch and ended with a more intimate meal in memory of ancestors on the third day. However, it is more practical these days to celebrate it in one day. Every stage of the ritual revolves around a bread called *colac*, a round loaf, braided and usually very ornate. People make flowers, birds, crosses, leaves and fruit shapes from extra bread dough to adorn the loaf before baking, but you can make it as simple or as intricate as you wish. I tested a recipe that is good for a beginner baker while still keeping the spirit of the occasion (see page 78). After the loaf is blessed by the priest, it can be sliced in four, then each quarter placed on the four corners of the table with a candle. Other families prefer to tear the bread together and share it without using the knife for slicing. The rest of the feast has roast meats served with a tomato sauce called *paradaisă*, and rice pilaf, stuffed cabbage rolls and sweets. If Praznic falls on a Wednesday or a Friday, when Orthodox people observe Lent, then all the dishes must be vegan.

The Serbian cuisine in the Iron Gates Banat is a reflection of the many centuries of living together with Romanians, Germans and Hungarians. Many recipes dotted throughout this book speak of this shared legacy, I hope you'll enjoy them.

The chapter that follows is about dishes you can have at breakfast or brunch: poppy seed pancakes, savoury bread and butter pudding, polenta (cornmeal) with eggs, baked cheese, eggs with leeks as well as smoked mackerel spread.

Cașcaval Pané

BREADED CHEESE WITH TARTAR SAUCE

A popular dish in Romanian restaurants, this is rich enough to be served on its own for breakfast and with fries for lunch. This type of fried breaded cheese is found in many countries across the Balkans, and in some it is served with a tartar sauce. It comes together quickly, so be ready to eat it while warm and the cheese still soft. The coating turns into a gorgeous, crackly crust, and the sound of the fork cutting through the first morsel is very enticing.

Serves 2

For the Tartar Sauce

100 g (3½ oz/generous ⅓ cup)
  mayonnaise
1 small pickled gherkin,
  finely diced
1 thin spring onion (scallion),
  finely sliced
1 teaspoon chopped dill,
  tarragon or parsley
salt and freshly ground black
  pepper, to taste

For the Fried Cheese

sunflower or vegetable oil,
  for frying
240 g (9oz) block of Romanian
  cașcaval or medium Cheddar
1 medium egg, beaten
50 g (2 oz/generous ½ cup)
  fine golden breadcrumbs

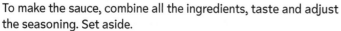

To make the sauce, combine all the ingredients, taste and adjust the seasoning. Set aside.

Cover the base of a frying pan (skillet) with a generous amount of oil and heat well. Cut the cheese into 6 slices on the shorter side of the block. They should be around 0.8–1cm (⅓–½ in) thick and 40 g (1½ oz) each. Dip them in the egg on both sides, making sure there are no dry patches, then toss and coat them in the breadcrumbs.

Carefully place the cheese slices in the oil and fry for 1½ minutes on each side over a medium heat until golden and crisp.

Serve immediately with the sauce. You can also add a fried egg, chips and a tomato salad to make it into a lunch dish.

Notes on Tartar and Tarator

Throughout the Balkans, yoghurt dishes using the excellent quality of traditional dairy produce are very popular. There are many variations, which can be confusing, and one name springs to mind as an example: *tarator*. In Bulgaria, a *tarator* is a drink or a soup, made with grated or diced fresh cucumbers, yoghurt, walnuts, garlic, salt, sunflower oil, fresh dill and some water. When it is served without water and the consistency is thicker, the same ingredients make a Snow White Salad or a dry *tarator*. In the winter, when fresh cucumbers and dill are not available, people use

pickled gherkins and dried dill, in which case they make a Thracian Salad. In Greece, the yoghurt and cucumber salad is called tzatziki, made with mint and no walnuts, and the cucumbers are squeezed of most of their water, making a thick and spreadable dip. In Romania, the closest dish is *scordolea*, after the Greek name for garlic (see page 92), but uses stale bread, garlic, milk and walnuts, similar to a Turkish *taratorlu*. Whatever the versions and ingredients, *tarator* is a good dish to serve with fried fish or vegetables.

Sf. Elena Livenci

ST. HELENA YEASTED PANCAKES WITH POPPY SEEDS

When I visited the Czech ethnic villages in Romania, I stayed for one night in St. Helena, or Svatá Helena as the locals call it. The winding road climbing up to it offered one of the most spectacular views of the Danube. For breakfast, my host showed me how to prepare these pancakes made with yeasted batter. She made them quite thin and topped them with poppy seeds, an important ingredient in the area, cooked in milk with honey.

Serves 4

150 g (5 oz/ 1 ¼ cups)
    plain (all-purpose) flour
15 g (½ oz/ 1 tablespoon)
    caster (superfine) sugar
7 g (1 sachet) fast-action
    dried yeast
1 medium egg
135 ml (4½ fl oz/generous
    ½ cup) full-fat milk
1 pinch of salt
sunflower or vegetable oil,
    for frying

For the Topping

25 g (1 oz) unsalted butter,
    plus extra to serve
80 g (3 oz/¾ cup) poppy seeds
180 ml (6 fl oz/¾ cup)
    full-fat milk
35 ml (1 fl oz/generous 2
    tablespoons) runny honey,
    plus extra to serve

In a large bowl, combine the flour, sugar and yeast, then make a well in the middle. In a separate bowl, beat the egg with the milk and salt. Pour the egg mixture into the well in the flour mixture and gradually mix everything together using a fork. Cover and allow to rise in a warm place for 40 minutes until it looks bubbly.

Make the topping by melting the butter in a small pan. Add the poppy seeds and cook until they start to release their nutty aroma. Stir in the milk and simmer gently until the mixture thickens. Take it off the heat and mix in the honey.

Cover the base of a frying pan (skillet) with a very thin layer of cooking oil and heat well. Use a serving or salad spoon to scoop the batter into the pan to form 2–3 pancakes. Keep the heat on medium so they don't burn, and cook for 1–2 minutes on each side. Peek under the pancakes to check if they are golden brown, then flip them onto their other sides. When cooked, remove to a plate lined with paper towel and rub some butter on top while they are still hot. Keep the plate covered with kitchen foil while you prepare the rest.

Serve immediately, topped with generous spoonfuls of the poppy seed topping and a good drizzle of honey.

Papară

SAVOURY BREAD AND BUTTER PUDDING
WITH BACON

A *papară* describes a dish where the ingredients are mashed together to a soft texture. It is a peasant dish, often using up stale bread or leftover ingredients. It has entered urban kitchens due to how easy and practical it is. In Romania, it involves eggs, to which we can add milk, cheese, lardons, sausages and bread. The result is a creamy dish where the flavours blend quickly. In other countries south of the Danube, it can be just milk and stale bread topped with cheese, a sprinkle of paprika and a dot of butter. Whatever the version, it is a clever way to turn simple ingredients into something unpretentious and utterly delicious.

Serves 4

25 ml (scant 2 tablespoons) sunflower or vegetable oil
6 thin rashers of back bacon
200 g (7 oz) stale bread or baguette
25 g (1 oz) salted butter
220 ml (8 fl oz/scant 1 cup) full-fat milk
4 medium eggs, beaten
50 g (2 oz) Romanian *cașcaval* or Cheddar, grated
freshly ground black pepper
½ teaspoon chopped thyme

Heat the oil in a 23 cm (9 in) non-stick frying pan (skillet). Slice the bacon across into wide pieces and cook over a medium heat to avoid burning until the edges turn crisp. Transfer to a plate.

Cut the bread or baguette into 2 cm (¾ in) slices, then each slice into 4 pieces. Fry them in the remaining fat in the pan along with the butter, keeping the heat on medium-low so they don't burn. When the crusts turn golden, add the milk and stir for about 3 minutes for the milk to be absorbed slowly. Pour over the beaten eggs and cheese, stir and shake the pan a few times. After 1 minute, when the eggs look creamy, add the bacon back to the pan, season with pepper, combine and turn the heat off. Leave it for 30 seconds, then transfer to a serving dish, sprinkle the thyme on top and take it to the table.

Note

You can cook it until the eggs are completely set and firm, but you will lose the silky, smooth texture of the dish.

Ouă cu Praz

EGGS WITH SAUTÉED LEEKS AND COURGETTES

This breakfast dish celebrates Oltenia's culinary symbol: the leek. The region is in southern Romania, where people use leeks, especially their green tops, to make dishes that have a delicate sweetness and a vibrant colour. More about this cuisine on page 97.

Serves 2

25 ml (scant 2 tablespoons) sunflower or vegetable oil, plus extra as needed
100 g (3½ oz) finely sliced leeks, green tops included
120 g (4 oz) courgettes (zucchini), grated
1 medium garlic clove, grated
2 medium eggs
salt and freshly ground black pepper

Heat the oil in a 20 cm (8 in) frying pan (skillet) over a medium heat, add the leeks and a generous pinch of salt, and fry for 5 minutes until they soften. Stir in the courgettes and garlic, season again, then add another splash of oil if necessary and cook for 2 more minutes.

Make two wells in the mixture, add a drizzle of oil to each, then crack in the eggs. Fry until the egg whites are cooked and the yolks are still runny. Try to scoop some of the hot oil from the pan over the yolks and whites so they cook evenly. Shake the pan if you think the mixture is catching on the base.

Serve immediately with a sprinkle of ground pepper.

Roșii cu Ouă

TOMATO SCRAMBLED EGGS WITH POTTED CHEESE

This dish is often called Bulgarian omelette because Bulgarians in Romania are renowned vegetable growers. Read more about that on page 85. Tomatoes are the dominant ingredient in this recipe and are cooked briefly prior to adding the eggs, to release their sweetness and lose some of their acidity. I serve the dish with one of my favourite potted cheese recipes, *urdă cu mărar,* made with dill, which is citrussy and refreshing.

Serves 2

For the Potted Cheese

100 g (3½ oz) *urdă*, curd cheese, or Wensleydale cheese
80 g (3 oz/scant ⅓ cup) full-fat yoghurt
25 g (1 oz) salted butter, softened
2 tablespoons finely chopped dill

For the Eggs

25 ml (scant 2 tablespoons) sunflower or vegetable oil
1 medium brown onion, finely sliced
10 small cherry tomatoes, quartered
2 large eggs, beaten
salt and freshly ground black pepper

To Serve

toast

Start with the potted cheese. Use a fork or a food processor to crumble the cheese. Add the yoghurt and butter, and blend to a creamy, spreadable consistency. Mix in the dill, transfer to a bowl and set aside.

Heat the oil in a 23 cm (9 in) frying pan over a medium heat, add the onions with a generous pinch of salt and cook until the onions start to caramelise. Mix in the tomatoes and cook for 5 more minutes until soft but not mushy. Reduce the heat to low, add the eggs and more salt, and stir a couple of times to distribute the tomatoes evenly throughout the eggs. Leave for 10 seconds, then stir again. Repeat two more times, then season and serve while the eggs still look creamy and are not fully set.

Serve with slices of good bread, toasted and spread with the potted cheese.

Mămăligă de Mei cu Lapte

MILLET PORRIDGE WITH MILK AND JAM

I make this dish whenever I want something comforting and uplifting for breakfast. I use cornmeal or millet, the latter being the ancient staple grain of Europe for preparing any nourishing meals similar to porridge. It is also the ancestor of Romanian cornmeal polenta. Even in the 20th century, some villages in Dobrogea, southern Romania, still used millet to prepare a traditional pudding for Whitsun celebrations. I think millet, with its nutty flavour, is perfect for sweet dishes.

Serves 2

200 g (7 oz/1⅓ cups) hulled millet
450 ml (15 fl oz/1¾ cups) full-fat milk, plus extra to serve
50 g (2 oz/¼ cup) caster (superfine) sugar
1 pinch of salt
45 g (1¾ oz) unsalted butter
plum, cherry or your favourite jam, to serve
ground cinnamon, for dusting

Put the millet, milk, sugar and salt in a pan, and gently bring to the boil. Turn the heat to medium-low, cover and simmer for 20 minutes.

Stir in the butter and serve immediately, pouring more milk around it in the bowl. Top with as much jam as you like and dust with cinnamon.

Salată de Pește Afumat

SMOKED MACKEREL SALAD

Smoked fish salad is a popular starter in Romania and is often made with mackerel. In the Danube Delta it can be made with *scrumbie de Dunăre afumată*, smoked Pontic shad from the herring family. It is famous in this region and has Protected Geographical Indication status.

Serves 4

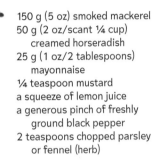

150 g (5 oz) smoked mackerel
50 g (2 oz/scant ¼ cup)
    creamed horseradish
25 g (1 oz/2 tablespoons)
    mayonnaise
¼ teaspoon mustard
a squeeze of lemon juice
a generous pinch of freshly
    ground black pepper
2 teaspoons chopped parsley
    or fennel (herb)

To Serve (optional)

olives
sliced red onion
boiled eggs

First, remove the skin on the back of each mackerel fillet. Place the fillets in a bowl and use a fork to tear them up into thin shreds. Add the rest of the ingredients, except the herbs, and mix well. Taste and adjust the flavours, especially the tanginess from the lemon, and the pepper. Transfer to a serving bowl and scatter the parsley on top. Chill in the refrigerator for 2 hours, so the flavours infuse and the horseradish mellows.
    Serve with olives, slices of red onion and boiled eggs.

Eibenthal Village and Potato Pancakes with Horseradish Cream and Gherkins

This is a popular dish at a little Czech restaurant in the Romanian Banat region near the Danube. It is called Eibenthal, after the name of the village. The savoury pancakes are made following the traditional Czech method: flat and spread to match the size of the plate they are served on. In Eibenthal, they come with garlic mousse or with gherkins and horseradish. When you visit the village, you must stop here for the traditional food (and beer!). They have an amazing menu, and these pancakes look fabulous.

The Czechs were the last ethnic groups to settle in Romania in the 19th century, mostly in the southern part of the Banat overlooking the Danube Gorge. They were lured here by a Hungarian entrepreneur to fell trees, with the promise that they could keep the land. The first two villages, St. Elisabeta and St. Helena, were named after his daughters, but sadly the promises proved to be false and vanished into thin air 'like the steam over the pot', as the Czechs say. However, the Austrian authorities who were ruling over the Banat in those times liked the idea of logging – after all, trees and land were only valuable if they brought income to the Austrian Crown. So, they invited more Czechs, offering tax exemptions, property and ready-built houses where they could settle right away. They came and stayed, becoming Romanians when the country gained its independence in the 20th century, and kept working in forestry, mining and local industry. When the Communist regime collapsed in 1989, it took everything down with it, and people lost their jobs. Many Romanian Czechs returned to the newly formed Czech Republic when it split from Czechoslovakia in 1993. Others stayed, but what was left to do?

Years later, four friends – returned sons of the village – thought of tourism as a way to save their own communities. They opened a guesthouse, then a brewery to make the fantastic Czech beer, then a place to eat, and – why not – a music festival. Hundreds of people come to these villages every August for something that looks like Oktoberfest crossed with Glastonbury. There is even a direct train, 18 carriages leaving Prague and passing through Brno, clickety-clack over 1,000 km to Orşova station in Romania, bringing tourists to stay with the locals. It's a Czech-speaking event, just like the Eisteddfod is an event for Welsh speakers in the UK, but there is something universal about it.

If you enjoy singing, partying, drinking Czech beer and eating traditional Czech food from the Banat, I reckon you'll be fine even if you don't speak the language.

I visited in quieter times, in September, and I was greeted in English, then Czech, so when I looked puzzled they finally said in Romanian, 'Sorry, there are so many tourists around...' The restaurant was busy offering comfort food to see you through the day. Dishes with silky dumplings soaking up the sauces, ham hock baked in beer served with jacket potatoes, a creamy garlic soup, and an interesting tripe soup topped with grated cheese were skilfully prepared by women in the village. For breakfast, I had yeasted pancakes served with poppy seeds, and buns topped with jam and curd cheese. You will discover those recipes on pages 30 and 234, but first try these potato pancakes (see page 42).

Plăcinte Eibenthal

EIBENTHAL POTATO PANCAKES WITH HORSERADISH CREAM AND GHERKINS

Serves 2

Grate the potatoes and mix them with white wine vinegar and 1 teaspoon salt, leaving them for 10 minutes. This will prevent them from turning brown.

Meanwhile, beat the eggs, slice the spring onions, and grate the garlic.

Working in small batches, squeeze as much liquid as you can from the potatoes and place them in a separate bowl. Mix them with the beaten eggs, cheese, flour, spring onions, garlic, and another teaspoon of salt.

Heat 30 ml of oil in a 20cm diameter frying pan (skillet). Add half the batter to the pan and use the back of the spoon to spread it evenly across the base. Keep the heat on medium-high and fry for five minutes, shaking the pan occasionally. The top will still be soft, but the base will be set enough to slide the pancake onto a plate. Place another plate on top, then turn it over. Slide the pancake back into the pan and cook for another minute, then remove it onto a serving plate and keep it warm in a low-temperature oven. Repeat with the remaining batter and serve the pancakes immediately with horseradish cream and pickled gherkins.

350 g (12 oz) potatoes, washed and skin on
1 tablespoon white wine vinegar
2 teaspoons salt
4 large eggs
4 thin spring onions (scallions)
1 large garlic clove
20 g (¾ oz/2 heaped tablespoons) plain (all-purpose) flour
35 g (1¼ oz) Cheddar, grated
60 ml (2 fl oz/¼ cup) oil, for frying

To Serve

1 small jar of horseradish cream (use as much as you like)
1 small jar of pickled gherkins or cornichons

Ouă Fierte cu Sos de Smântână

BOILED EGGS WITH SOUR CREAM SAUCE AND PAPRIKA ONIONS

This is an elegant dish from the culinary past of southern Romania, where Walachian *boyars* (nobility) in country manors (*conace*), hosted feasts for the pleasure of eating. It gets its flavours from layering the boiled eggs with sour cream, then topping them with piquant, caramelised onions.

Serves 4

 4 medium eggs
thickly sliced bread, to serve

For the Sour Cream Sauce

35 g (1¼ oz) salted butter
1 tablespoon plain
  (all-purpose) flour
250 g (9 oz/1 cup) sour cream

For the Paprika Onions

50 ml (1¾ fl oz/3 tablespoons)
  sunflower or vegetable oil
1 medium brown onion, sliced
a pinch of salt
1 teaspoon salted butter
½ teaspoon paprika

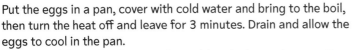

Put the eggs in a pan, cover with cold water and bring to the boil, then turn the heat off and leave for 3 minutes. Drain and allow the eggs to cool in the pan.

Meanwhile, make the sauce by melting the butter in a small pan. Stir in the flour, cook for a further minute, then add the sour cream and combine well. Keep on a very low heat while you are making the caramelised paprika onions.

Heat the oil in a medium frying pan (skillet) over a medium heat, add the onions and a pinch of salt and cook until golden. Stir them often so they don't burn. Add the butter and paprika, stir everything together until the butter is melted, then turn the heat off.

Peel the eggs, slice them in half and arrange in a shallow bowl. Pour the sauce over and sprinkle with the onions. Serve warm with thick slices of bread.

Brânză la Cuptor

BULGARIAN BAKED CHEESE

A popular Bulgarian dish in its own country south of the Danube and also in neighbouring Romania north of the Danube, it is known as *Sirene po Shopski*. Petya Borisova, whose grandfather came from a village very close to the Danube, told me that many Bulgarians prefer to prepare it with tinned tomatoes, even when tomatoes are in season. I think that fresh tomatoes are best eaten in salads.

Serves 2 as a sharing dish

200 g (7 oz/generous ¾ cup) tinned chopped tomatoes
2 tablespoons olive oil
250 g (9 oz) Bulgarian or feta-style cheese
salt and freshly ground black pepper
sliced bread, to serve

Preheat the oven to 180°C fan (350°F/gas 4).

Spread half of the tomatoes evenly over the base of a 16–18 cm (6¼–7 in) baking dish and season with salt and pepper. Drizzle 1 tablespoon of the olive oil on top, place the block of cheese in the middle and cover it with the rest of the tomatoes. Season and drizzle with the remaining olive oil. Bake on a higher shelf for 20 minutes.

Serve hot with slices of bread.

Note

Although not traditional to this dish in Bulgaria, I found similar recipes from the Balkans where the cheese is blended with milk and a little flour before baking.

Mămăligă la Cuptor

BAKED CORNMEAL WITH SOUR CREAM, CHEESE AND EGGS

This dish will bring comfort and a sunny mood to your morning. It is nicknamed 'shut up and eat' because it's best eaten hot. It is often made with a whole, cracked egg on top, but I prefer to use beaten eggs for the extra-smooth texture. There is more about the importance of maize and cornmeal (polenta) in Romanian cuisine on page 13.

Serves 2

500 ml (17 fl oz/2 cups) water
2 teaspoons salt, plus an extra pinch for baking
150 g (5 oz/1 cup) fine cornmeal (polenta)
45 g (1¾ oz) salted butter, plus extra for dotting
75 g (2½ oz) *cașcaval* or Cheddar, grated, plus extra for baking
200 g (7 oz/generous ¾ cup) sour cream
2 medium eggs, beaten
1 teaspoon chopped fresh thyme

Preheat the oven to 180°C fan (350°F/gas 4) or the grill (broiler) to maximum temperature.

In a deep pan, bring the measured water and salt to the boil. Add the cornmeal and use a whisk to distribute it evenly in the water. Reduce the heat to low, cover and allow the cornmeal to absorb the liquid for 8–10 minutes. Whisk a couple of times throughout this process.

Stir in the butter and cheese, then pour the cornmeal into a 23 cm (9 in) ceramic baking dish. Allow it to cool a little, then make a large well in the middle. Add the sour cream, sprinkle with a pinch of salt, then add the beaten eggs, working them a little with a fork into the sour cream. Place a few dots of butter on top and another sprinkle of grated cheese. Bake or grill (broil) for 10 minutes, or until the eggs are just set and the cornmeal has a beautiful golden crust.

Sprinkle the thyme on top and serve hot.

A LAND

OF
MILLERS

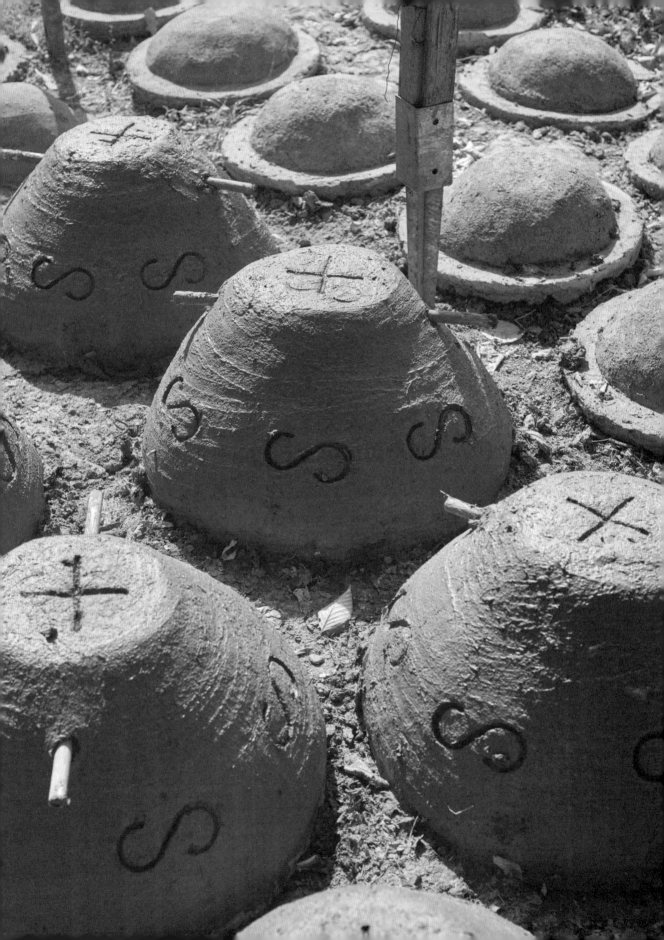

Oltenian Ash Bread

'We've turned this childhood memory into a mission for saving an endangered tradition of țest building and bread making,' said George Dumitru and Daniel Popa, the owners of Țesturi Pâine. It sounds simple, but I know the realities behind these words. Many Romanians pursue their dream of returning to the countryside and saving our cultural heritage, but to be a small entrepreneur is an act of courage and a feat of survival against bureaucracy and provincial attitudes. 'We still have to have a job in the city to keep this business going, but you measure success in a different way. If your family is proud of you, if our children grow up proud of their roots, if you see people reconnecting with their past, that's your biggest achievement,' says George.

A țest (tzest) speaks of a way of life in southern Romania, especially in one of its regions called Oltenia, where it has been used since Roman times for two millennia. It is a clay cloche that people use for baking bread and cooking. The word țest comes from the Latin *testum*, and I asked Farrell Monaco, a classical archaeologist who specialises in the food preparation of the Graeco-Roman Mediterranean, about it. 'These baking vessels, usually just a cover or a cover and a base, were typically used in the republican Roman period in domestic settings. It's a closed, domed, ceramic baking environment that bakes bread as efficiently as possible with no heat loss,' writes Farrell.

It is also cheaper to heat than a classic outdoor oven since you only need some twigs, weeds, dried sunflower stalks or corn cobs. In the past, this was a huge advantage when fuel was sparse. It was also portable if you needed it in a field or anywhere else on bare ground. The bread was usually placed straight on the embers and covered with the dome, with more hot embers placed around it. Romans popularised this system in Romania and the Balkans, and it has survived as a daily bread-making way in Oltenia, southern Romania. 'It's fascinating to hear that a Romanian bread is still made the way it was 2,000 years ago!' says Farrell, and I share her enthusiasm.

Even before the Romans had arrived in Oltenia, the Dacian and Getae tribes, the ancestors of Romanians today, were growing millet, barley and wheat. Historical sources as old as the 5th century BC mention the excellent leavened bread that people ate in the region. This attracted the Romans' attention. Also, the soil quality allowed the making of pottery, as many archaeological discoveries from Neolithic times prove. So, the South had the wheat fields to make excellent bread and the clay to build a good *testum* for baking.

'In the old days, this țest was built only by women and only on certain days after Easter, called *Ropotinul Țestelor*,' says George. 'A whole magic ritual surrounded it, where the kneading and shaping of the clay were interspersed with incantations meant to protect the wheat crops.' George and Daniel don't whisper any mystic words when they build their ovens but follow George's grandmother's method, the person who inspired them to rescue this old tradition. 'We send them all over the world, mainly to fellow countrymen who long for the flavours of their childhood.' So, where was the most exotic delivery address, I wondered. 'To an Oltenian in South America,' he answered.

Pâine la Țest

OLTENIAN ASH BREAD

This recipe hails from Oltenia where the bread is made under an earthenware cloche called a *țest* (tzest). It has a direct lineage to ancient Rome, where baking was done under a *testu* or *clibanus* and placed into a wood-burning hearth. The cloche's sides and top were covered with hot embers to ensure good heat distribution. In Romania, it was traditional to place the țest on the bare ground, but in more modern times we've used flat, stone or brick surfaces. I have also seen it used inside the house, where the owners had an old, open fireplace and put the cloche in there. I've adapted the method for a standard oven to give similar results. The dough is pierced before baking so that it doesn't puff up and has a soft, slightly gooey crumb, utterly moreish when served warm.

Makes a 23 cm (9 in) loaf

350 g (12 oz/2¾ cups) strong
   bread flour
7 g (1 sachet) fast-action
   dried yeast
8 g (scant 1½ teaspoons)
   fine salt
225 ml (8 fl oz/scant 1 cup)
   lukewarm water
sunflower or olive oil,
   for greasing
1 tomato (optional)

Stir the flour, yeast, salt and water together in a bowl, cover and leave for 15 minutes.

On a lightly oiled work surface, knead the dough a few times until smooth, then roll it into a ball and place back in the bowl. Cover and leave for 1 hour.

Grease the base and sides of a 23 cm (9 in) non-stick, ovenproof pan with a lid (I use a heavy sauté pan) with oil. Place the dough in the middle and flatten it, pushing gently to cover the base of the pan. Cover with the lid and leave for 20 minutes.

Preheat the oven to 220°C fan (425°F/gas 7).

Brush the top of the bread with 1 tablespoon of oil and use a fork to prick it all over. I like to make a pattern like sun rays, leaving a small circle in the middle. Some people like to slice a tomato in half and rub it on the bread for a darker crust.

Put the lid on and place the pan in the oven on a middle rack. Bake for 35 minutes until the bread is lightly golden. Remove the lid and bake for 5 more minutes to get a darker colour on the crust, then transfer the bread to a cooling rack.

Eat it slightly warm or on the day you bake it.

Note

If you are using a bread cloche, you need to follow the manufacturer's instructions.

Plăcintă Dobrogeană

CHEESE PIE FROM DOBROGEA

This pie is the culinary symbol of Dobrogea and brings together two historic occupations: the miller and the shepherd. Dobrogea was once known as the Land of the Windmills, and the millers were known for producing high-quality flour required to stretch the filo pastry as thinly as a leaf. The shepherds, who moved their sheep flocks up and down the Carpathian pastures, were skilled at making *telemea*, a salty, tangy, and full-of-character cheese that was a statement ingredient in this celebratory pie.

In the past, the pie was made for New Year celebrations, since cheese and flour were symbols of regeneration, then during Cheesefare Week (a week before Easter Lent, when people eat dairy) and at weddings and christenings. Gradually, it travelled from the countryside into urban spaces and professional bakeries, becoming a staple pie you could get for a snack. When I set out to search for the authentic Dobrogeană through these lands, I saw it served in many different ways. People were saying, 'This is the real Dobrogeană,' I found it confusing and alarming that the original recipe had been lost among the rest of Romanian pies. Had it not been for a group of traditional bakers from Greci village, it could have easily been the case. They succeeded in gaining Protected Geographical Indication status and making the recipe official. Its main elements are freshly made filo pastry, filled with *telemea*, salty cheese and *caş*, mozzarella-style cheese. The filo is then crinkled, like a pleated skirt, swirled around itself, placed in a round baking tin and covered with crème fraîche mixed with eggs. After baking, the crust is soft and tender, as opposed to crispy and brittle, like in many other variations.

The recipe overleaf is my version using ingredients easily accessible outside of Romania.

Serves 6–8

Preheat the oven to 160°C fan (310°F/gas 2). Use a 25–26 cm (10–10½ in) (measured at the top) enamel pie dish or ovenproof frying pan (skillet) to assemble the pie.

Make the filling by mixing all the ingredients.

Work with two filo sheets at a time, keeping the rest under a damp towel to avoid them drying out. Brush both sheets with oil and stack them, keeping a long side closest to you. Scatter a third of the cheese mixture on the bottom half of the pastry, then fold the other half over the filling and loosely gather the sheets together like a pleated skirt. Brush lightly with oil. Gently swirl it around itself in a spiral (it may crack in places but that's okay) and place in the middle of the baking dish. Repeat with another two sheets, pleating them and continuing the spiral from where you left it in the pan. Repeat with the last two sheets until the pie fits perfectly in the dish. Work gently and don't press on the pleats. Brush with any remaining oil.

Mix the crème fraîche with the egg and spread it over the pie. Bake on a lower shelf for 35 minutes or until golden on top.

Allow it to cool, slice and serve as a snack.

For the Filling

400 g (14 oz) *brânză telemea*, Greek-style cheese or salty cheese matured in brine, crumbled
125 g (4 oz) extra-mature Cheddar, grated
a pinch each of salt and freshly ground black pepper

For the Pie

6 sheets of filo pastry, 45 x 30 cm (18 x 12 in)
35 ml (generous 2 tablespoons) oil, for brushing

For the Topping

150 g (5 oz/scant ⅔ cup) crème fraîche
1 medium egg, beaten

Covrigi cu Șuncă

HAM BREAD LOOPS

In Romania, *covrigi* and *colaci* are street food staples that are also baked on special and religious occasions. The long-established method of shaping them is into a simple braided loop. Like anything popular, the recipe has many variations, either regional or modern, such as jam-filled or a savoury version with slices of *șuncă*, ham. Here is one of them.

Makes 8

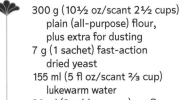

300 g (10½ oz/scant 2½ cups) plain (all-purpose) flour, plus extra for dusting
7 g (1 sachet) fast-action dried yeast
155 ml (5 fl oz/scant ⅔ cup) lukewarm water
30 ml (2 tablespoons) sunflower or vegetable oil
1 teaspoon salt

For the Filling

4 slices of ham, cut into strips

For Topping

1 egg, beaten
poppy or onion seeds

Make the dough by mixing all the ingredients in a bowl, making sure you add the salt last. Mix and knead for 4–5 minutes until the dough comes away from the sides of the bowl. Cover with a clean dish towel and leave in a warm place for 1 hour to prove until springy.

Preheat the oven to 180°C fan (350°F/gas 4). Line 1–2 baking sheets with baking parchment.

Dust the work surface and a rolling pin with flour, divide the dough into 8 balls and roll each into a rectangle about 30 x 12 cm (12 x 5 in).

Place strips of ham along one of the long edges, leaving a 2 cm (¾ in) gap at the ends and brush the dough with a little water. Starting from the long edge, roll into a cigar shape. Make into a loop by bringing both ends together and pinch to seal. Place on the prepared baking sheets, brush the loops with the beaten egg and sprinkle with poppy or onion seeds. Bake on a lower oven shelf for 15–20 minutes until lightly golden.

Remove from the oven and keep them under a clean dish towel. Serve warm as a snack.

Șuberec

FRIED LAMB PASTRIES WITH WATERMELON

These pies are traditional to the Tatar communities in Dobrogea (see page 197). In restaurants and Tatar homes, the pies are served with slices of watermelon in the summer and prune compôte in the winter. Otherwise, when they are sold in bakeries or *șuberec* huts lining the streets of the Black Sea resorts, they come with no extras.

These pastries are usually prepared on the spot and served hot. If not, Tatar women employ a little trick at home by adding baking powder to the dough, which keeps the pastries soft for longer. You know it's a good *șuberec* when the juices of the meat run through your fingers as you bite into the pastry.

Makes 4

Make the dough by combining all the ingredients in a bowl. Turn out onto the work surface, knead for 2 minutes, then invert the bowl over it and allow the dough to rest for 10 minutes.

Knead for another 2 minutes and rest it for another 10 minutes, then divide into 4 equal parts.

Meanwhile, make the filling by blending all the ingredients in a food processor (or by hand, in which case you'll have to dice the onion finely). Hot water binds the filling and is absorbed better by the meat than cold water.

On a lightly floured work surface, roll out one piece of dough to roughly the size of a 24 cm (9½ in) diameter plate. Invert the plate on top and trim the edge all around. Spread a quarter of the lamb mixture evenly over half of the pastry and fold the other half over to cover. Seal the edges by pressing with your fingers. Set aside on a lightly floured surface and repeat with the rest.

Heat a generous layer of oil on the base of a frying pan (skillet) large enough to accommodate one pastry over a medium heat. Fry the *șuberec* for 3 minutes on each side until golden. It will form dark golden patches, which is okay. Drain off excess oil on paper towel and place on a plate. Slide the plate inside a clean plastic bag and keep it sealed while you prepare the rest.

Serve the pies warm next to thick slices of watermelon.

For the Dough

300 g (10½ oz/scant 2½ cups) strong bread flour, plus extra for dusting
3 g (¾ teaspoon) baking powder
7 g (1 heaped teaspoon) fine salt
175 ml (6 fl oz/¾ cup) water

For the Filling

250 g (9 oz) minced (ground) lamb
1 small brown onion
½ teaspoon fine salt
½ teaspoon freshly ground black pepper
1 teaspoon chopped fresh mint
35 ml (generous 2 tablespoons) hot water
sunflower or vegetable oil, for frying

To Serve

4 thick watermelon slices

Note

The shape of the pies also indicates the filling: when they are folded like a half moon, the filling is lamb or potatoes. If the pastry is square and cut diagonally in four, it is filled with cheese and called *dort kesken*. If it is square and dusted with icing (powdered) sugar, it's a sweet pastry with no filling, called *katlama*.

Plăcintă cu Praz

LEEK AND RICE PIE

A *plăcintă* is the iconic Romanian pie baked in a rectangular tray and served cold as a snack. In this recipe I use puff pastry, *foitaj*, the way I found it prepared in some bakeries in Dobrogea. However, when made with filo and baked in round tins, it is associated with the Macedonian and Vlach ethnic groups in southern Romania. In spring, they prepare it with foraged plants such as nettles, dandelions, wild spinach and even beetroot leaves, which I'd love you to try if you find any. The rice is optional or replaced by cheese to give the filling more body and makes the pie easy to slice.

Makes 16 slices

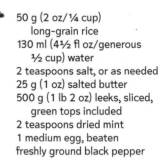

50 g (2 oz/¼ cup)
   long-grain rice
130 ml (4½ fl oz/generous
   ½ cup) water
2 teaspoons salt, or as needed
25 g (1 oz) salted butter
500 g (1 lb 2 oz) leeks, sliced,
   green tops included
2 teaspoons dried mint
1 medium egg, beaten
freshly ground black pepper

To Assemble

2 sheets of ready-rolled puff
   pastry, 35 x 23 cm (14 x 9 in)
1 medium egg, beaten
1 tablespoon sesame seeds,
   or more if wished

Boil the rice in the water with 1 teaspoon of the salt for 12–15 minutes until cooked, then set aside.

Preheat the oven to 180°C fan (350°F/gas 4).

Melt the butter in a large frying pan (skillet) over a medium heat, sprinkle the leeks with the remaining 1 teaspoon of salt and sauté them for 5 minutes, then add the rice and mint, and cook for another 5 minutes. You just want the leeks to soften while still retaining their crunch. If you decide to use fresh mint, add it at the end of the cooking time. Taste and adjust the seasoning. Set aside to cool a little, then mix in the egg.

Line a large-enough baking sheet to accommodate the pie and place one puff pastry sheet on it. Brush the edges with the egg wash and prick with a fork all over. Spoon the filling on top, leaving a narrow margin on all sides. Place the other pastry sheet on top and use the tines of a fork to seal the edges together. Prick the pastry all over, brush with some of the egg wash and sprinkle with sesame seeds (as much as you wish).

Bake for 15–20 minutes on a lower rack until golden brown. Remove from the oven and place a clean dish towel on top for 5 minutes, then leave to cool completely before slicing.

This is usually served cold, as a snack, and it keeps for a couple of days in the refrigerator.

Geantîc

TATAR BEEF BUNS WITH PLUM COMPOT

Another Tatar dish from Dobrogea, *geantîc* means 'to lean on'. It shows how the rolls are tucked in together, leaning on one another, keeping their sides soft while baking. It is traditional to brush them with a mixture of yoghurt and eggs, which forms a flavoursome and rich crust in the oven. Each of them is a little triumph. Although they are served after the soup dish, I like them as a snack or starter with a glass of chilled plum *compot*.

Makes 10 small rolls

Start by making the dough. Mix all the ingredients in a large bowl and knead until the dough looks smooth. It will be quite soft, which is fine. Cover the bowl and leave it in a warm place for 45 minutes.

Prepare the filling by heating a thin layer of oil in a frying pan (skillet) over a medium heat. Cook the onions with a pinch of salt until translucent and soft, then add the beef and cook for 15 minutes until the juices evaporate. Add the spices and a generous pinch of salt and pepper, then set aside.

Grease and line a 24 cm (9½ in) pie tin or ovenproof sauté pan, or sprinkle with flour.

Turn the dough out onto a lightly floured surface, then sprinkle more flour on top. Divide it into 10 equal balls, around 50 g (2 oz) each. If you want to be precise, weigh the dough first, divide by 10, then weigh each ball separately as you go along. Use a rolling pin to stretch one dough ball to an oval shape, around 10 x 8 cm (4 x 3 in). Place a generous spoonful of the filling in the middle, then stretch one side over the other like a dumpling. Turn it onto the seam, and bring the edges of your palms together underneath it, to seal it well. You should have an elongated 10 cm (4 in) bun. Place it in the prepared tin/pan and repeat with the rest. Arrange 4 buns in a vertical row in the middle of the dish, then 3 on each side, trying to leave a small gap between them.

Cover and leave in a warm place for 1 hour.

In the last 20 minutes, preheat the oven to 180°C fan (350°F/gas 4).

For the Dough

300 g (10½ oz/scant 2½ cups) strong bread flour, plus extra for dusting
5 g (¾ sachet) fast-action dried yeast
6 g (1 teaspoon) fine salt
½ teaspoon caster (superfine) sugar
50 g (2 oz/scant ¼ cup) full-fat Greek yoghurt
1 medium egg
130 ml (4½ fl oz/ generous ½ cup) water

For the Filling

sunflower or vegetable oil, for frying and greasing
1 large brown onion, sliced
280 g (10 oz) minced (ground) beef
½ teaspoon ground cumin
1 teaspoon sweet paprika
salt and freshly ground black pepper

For the Plum Compot

5 medium plums, stoned and quartered
300 ml (10 fl oz/ 1¼ cups) water
20 g (¾ oz/1½ tablespoons) caster (superfine) sugar
zest and juice of 1 large lemon

For Brushing

1 medium egg
20 g (¾ oz/1½ tablespoons) Greek-style yoghurt
1 tablespoon sesame seeds

Meanwhile, make the plum compôte by simmering all the ingredients together until the fruit is soft and starts to disintegrate. You can crush it lightly with a fork. Taste and add more lemon juice if needed; it doesn't have to be sweet. Set aside or place in the refrigerator to cool.

Beat the egg with the yoghurt and brush the buns with this mixture. Sprinkle sesame seeds on top and bake on a lower rack for 25 minutes. Cover with kitchen foil if the tops get too dark.

Remove from the oven, cover with a clean dish towel and leave to rest for 10 minutes before transferring to a cooling rack. Serve the buns warm with a glass of plum compôte.

Mălai Copt cu Hrean

YEASTED HORSERADISH CORNBREAD

Cornbread is something that all regions in Romania have in common, and many recipes use yeast and a combination of flour and cornmeal to give the bread more structure and flavour. They can be rectangular or round loaves and even individual cakes, like the ones prepared on St. Peter's Day at the end of June, which are baked on horseradish leaves. This is no coincidence, since in the summer the leaves are thick and large enough to protect the cakes from the direct heat of the oven. Here, I bring the flavours of the tradition together in a loaf that's light as a feather and golden as the sun.

Makes a 22 cm (8½ in) loaf

220 g (8 oz/1½ cups) medium-ground cornmeal (polenta)
335 ml (11¼ fl oz/1⅓ cups) hot, full-fat milk, plus extra if needed
160 g (5½ oz/1¼ cups) strong bread flour
7 g (1 sachet) fast-action dried yeast
9 g (1½ teaspoons) fine salt
40 ml (scant 3 tablespoons) sunflower oil
60 g (2¼ oz/¼ cup) horseradish cream
1 large egg
15 g (½ oz) unsalted butter, cubed, plus extra for greasing

Put the cornmeal in a large bowl, pour over the hot milk and mix well. Leave to absorb for no more than 10 minutes, then add the rest of the ingredients, apart from the butter. Use a spoon to combine them well. The mixture needs to have a very thick but still pourable consistency. If it is too dry, add more milk (you don't need to warm it). Cover the bowl with cling film (plastic wrap) and leave in a warm place for 1 hour.

Preheat the oven to 200°C fan (400°F/gas 6). Butter a 22 cm (8½ in) (external size) pie or cake tin, at least 5 cm (2 in) deep. Sprinkle the base and sides with flour.

Pour or spoon the cornmeal mixture into the tin and gently level the top. Bake for 20–22 minutes on a lower rack until golden. Remove to a cooling rack, rub some butter on top and serve slightly warm. It keeps for one extra day, and you can toast or fry it.

Oltenian Defence Towers, Cula Curtişoara and Oltenian Wine and Cornmeal Crackers

Oltenia is a region in historic Walachia, southern Romania, bordered at the top by the Carpathian Mountains and at the bottom by the Danube River, the latter also separating it from the Balkans. Here, the countryside is studded with 18th-century fortified towers, called *cule*, that were used for refuge and defence against raids. Hoards of bandits were crossing the Danube from the Balkans into this region, plundering villages in search of grain, food and wine.

Local landlords, called *boieri*, took inspiration from traditional houses and built *cule*. With metre-thick walls and an elevated ground level, the towers had a single entrance secured by a fortified door. At the top, there was an open gallery from where people were able to fight back. However, the fortifications were light, kitted up to ward off a bunch of thieves rather than to halt an army.

'The towers could have also been observation points,' says Pierre Bortnowski, French architect and owner of Curtişoara, 'being the only high buildings in the area, together with the church bell towers, they could have played a signalling and communication role between villages.' The name of this type of building is of Ottoman origin, *cule* meaning 'towers' in Turkish. 'The particularity in Romania is that they are built with bricks and rendered with lime wash, while in the neighbouring Balkans they are made of stone and left bare,' says Pierre.

The country saw a cultural and economic boom after the monarchy was established in Romania in 1866. *Cule* were expanded and converted into homes owned by cosmopolitan people inspired by their travels around the world. Cula Curtişoara was bought in 1927 by Pierre's great-grandfather Constantin Neamţu for its historical value. He made some improvements by building a water tower for running water and supplying it with electricity, which was remarkable at that time in rural Romania. He was one of the prominent political figures of Craiova, the capital of Oltenia, and a banker, founding the Commercial Bank, whose building is the City Hall today.

After WWII, the Communist party nationalised all private properties, including Curtişoara, from where they lifted all art collections down to every single furniture item and replaced them with farm animals and fodder. The party sent Neamţu to prison, where he later died, and persecuted his descendants for many years to follow. In the end, Pierre's father had to flee to Paris, but the family returned after the fall of the political regime.

'We returned home to Curtişoara,' says Pierre, 'to start the renovation project, which lasted a long time, even though we come from a long-established family of architects. We opened it up to international summer workshops where architecture students from France, Belgium and Romania learnt building and restoration techniques while working on this *cula* and also repairing the local school.'

Pierre is involved in many projects to preserve the local heritage. 'I want to bring more life into the old buildings, make them functional. A building, if you don't live in it, it's lifeless, and it will disappear not only physically but also from the collective memory.'

I wanted to learn more about the lifestyle of those who owned *cule* in the interwar period, but we don't have many written sources about their dinners and parties. Luckily, during a recent restoration of another *cula* done by the Pro Patrimonio Foundation, the team found an old notebook with recipes. *Maria Cantili Golescu, 20 recipes from 1900* is now a booklet you can access online, peeking into a past hidden for centuries. Franche-Comté Biscuits with Cornmeal, Tomato Glacé, Strawberry Mousse, Rice Cakes and Chiffonnette Cake are only a few examples. If these dishes could inspire today's chefs to gently and sympathetically adapt them to local ingredients, they could easily be a Romanian 'neo-boyar' cuisine, as in the recipe that follows.

Biscuiți Oltenești cu Vin

OLTENIAN WINE AND CORNMEAL CRACKERS

Makes 25 crackers

Use a food processor with a blade attachment to blend together the cornmeal, flour and butter to a coarse consistency. Add the rest of the ingredients and pulse a few times until they form a rough, sticky dough. Turn it out onto a piece of cling film (plastic wrap), press it down and roll it into an 18 cm (7 in) log, 4–5 cm (1½–2 in) in diameter. Put it in the freezer while you wait for the oven to heat.

Preheat the oven to 160°C fan (310°F/gas 2).

Cut the log into 3 mm (⅛ in) slices if you want them crispy and thin, or 5–8 mm (¼–⅜ in) slices if you want them to resemble a biscuit. Make sure all the slices are the same thickness and place on a baking sheet.

Bake for 12–14 minutes, then transfer to a cooling rack.

75 g (2½ oz/½ cup) fine cornmeal (polenta)
100 g (3½ oz/generous ¾ cup) plain (all-purpose) flour
60 g (2¼ oz) salted butter
100 g (3½ oz) Romanian *cașcaval* or extra-mature Cheddar, grated
40–60 ml (scant 3 tablespoons) dry white wine

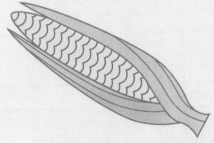

Trigoane cu Ceapă și Nucă

FILO PASTRIES WITH ONIONS AND WALNUTS

A staple street food snack, a *trigon* is a triangular pastry filled with anything from meat to fruit. This filling with onions and walnuts comes from the Muslim communities in Constanța, Dobrogea. It can be used in a rectangular pie if made at home, or – for portability reasons – in individual triangular pastries. Many traditional dishes from their cuisine in Dobrogea are turned into street food staples by simply adapting their shape.

Makes 12 medium pastries

50 ml (1¾ fl oz/3 tablespoons)
    sunflower oil
4 large brown onions,
    finely sliced
½ teaspoon salt
150 g (5 oz/1½ cups)
    shelled walnuts, chopped
a splash of milk, full-fat
    or plant-based
3 sheets of filo pastry,
    36 x 20 cm (14 x 8 in)
onion seeds, to decorate

Heat a thin layer of the oil in a frying pan (skillet) over a medium heat, add the onions with the salt and coat them well in the oil. Cook for 15–20 minutes until the onions are very soft, stirring often to avoid burning. Add the walnuts and a splash of milk to bind everything together into a rough paste. Set aside.

Preheat the oven to 170°C fan (325°F/gas 3). Line a large baking sheet or two, and work in batches.

Take one filo sheet and brush evenly with oil. Keeping the long side closest to you, cut it in half vertically, then cut each half in half again. Place a spoonful of the mixture in the bottom, right-hand corner of one ribbon. Lift the corner diagonally towards your left, forming a triangle. Lift the bottom left corner and flip the triangle over, then flip it to the right and over the top again. Once you start shaping them, you will see how easy it is – the pastry practically folds itself. Place it on the baking sheet and brush it with oil. Repeat with the rest of the filo ribbons and sheets.

Sprinkle the pastries with onion seeds and bake for 15 minutes on a middle shelf until golden.

Serve warm while the pastry is still crispy. They are also good cold, with the pastry slightly softer.

Note

If you work with two baking sheets, put one in the oven while shaping the pastries for the other.

Colac de Praznic

SVINIȚA FESTIVE BREAD

This is a festive bread from Sviniţa, one of the Romanian-Serbian villages in the Iron Gates region. It is baked for the annual Praznic celebrations, which are dedicated to the Saint Protector of the House. After the blessing at church, every member of the family holds a little corner of this loaf, tearing it apart together, reasserting and renewing their bond for another year.

Makes a 600 g (1 lb 5 oz) loaf

400 g (14 oz/3 ¼ cups) strong bread flour
10 g (1½ sachets) fast-action dried yeast
½ teaspoon caster (superfine) sugar
5 g (1 teaspoon) fine salt
225 ml (8 fl oz/scant 1 cup) lukewarm full-fat milk
30 g (1 oz) unsalted butter, melted
20 ml (1½ tablespoons) sunflower oil, plus extra for greasing
1 medium egg, separated

Mix the dry ingredients in a bowl, then add the milk, butter, oil and egg white. Knead for 10 minutes until the dough is smooth and comes away from the sides of the bowl. Cover and leave in a warm place for 1 hour. It is a soft dough at this stage, which is okay and will make a light bread.

Grease a 23 cm (9 in) baking or pie tin (not ceramic) and line the base only with baking parchment.

Separate a 90 g (3 ¼ oz) piece of dough and roll it into a ball. Place it in the middle of the tin. Divide the rest of the dough into 3 equal parts and roll each into a 75 cm (30 in) long strand. Turn the strands perpendicular to you and pinch together the ends at the top. Lift the right strand and place it between the other two. Now lift the left strand and place it between the other two. Keep doing this until you have braided it all together. Trim both ends, then place the wreath in the tin around the dough in the middle without touching the sides of the tin or the bun. You can overlap the ends if necessary, ensuring the wreath has the same thickness all round. Cover and leave in a warm place for 45 minutes.

In the last 20 minutes, preheat the oven to 200°C fan (400°F/ gas 6).

Whisk the egg yolk with 1 tablespoon of water and brush the bread thoroughly with the mixture. Bake for 20 minutes on the lower shelf until beautifully golden.

Păsări

LOVE BREADS

Dragobete is our Romanian Valentine's Day celebrated on 24 February. It usually involves the first flowers of spring, water from melted snow and stealing a kiss from the girl you'd like to marry. In many ways, it is a day full of anticipation and new bonds, and further down the line, the wedding day is celebrated by baking bread shaped like birds. After all, it is a nesting ritual. I've gathered together all these independent elements in a recipe for finding new love.

Pro tip: Make the bread really salty and eat it before you go to bed. Your chosen one will appear in your dream, bringing you water to quench your thirst.

Makes 8 buns

375 g (13 oz/3 cups) strong bread flour
7 g (1 sachet) fast-action dried yeast
8 g (scant 1½ teaspoons) fine salt
225 ml (8 fl oz/scant 1 cup) lukewarm water
15 g (½ oz) lard or unsalted butter, melted
2 teaspoons dried basil
2 tablespoons full-fat milk or 1 small beaten egg
onion seeds, to decorate

To Brush after Baking

1 tablespoon finely chopped fresh basil
1 tablespoon sunflower or olive oil
½ teaspoon salt

Combine the flour, yeast, salt and water in a bowl, add the lard or butter and basil, and knead until the dough looks smooth. Cover and leave in a warm place for 1 hour.

Divide the dough into 8 equal pieces. Roll one into a 32 cm (13 in) rope, then make a loose knot. One end will be the tail of the bird, the other will be the head. Place the bird on its belly, lift and push the 'neck' and 'head' down towards the middle of the body. Pinch the very end of it to form a beak. Repeat to make 8 birds and place on a baking sheet. Cover and leave in a warm place for 30 minutes.

Preheat the oven to 180°C fan (350°F/gas 4). Mix the basil, oil and salt for brushing and set aside.

Reshape the beaks if necessary, then gently brush each bird with the milk or beaten egg. Stick a tiny onion seed on each side of the head to make the eyes. Elongate the tail a little. Bake for 12–15 minutes on a lower shelf, or until the crust turns golden.

Remove the breads from the oven and brush them with the basil oil while still hot. Serve warm.

Note

To make the 'birds in a nest' shape, divide the last piece of dough in half. Roll each to the necessary length to encircle two birds together, then twist into a rope and place around the breads. Not too tight, as the dough needs to expand.

A LAND

TO
SHARE

Bulgarian Communities of Vegetable Growers

To think of Eastern European cuisine as one abundant in vegetable dishes requires a mindset change for many of us. Let's be honest, vegetables don't spring to mind when we sit down at the table in Eastern Europe and the Balkans. It is often the case that, as tourists, we can only experience the dishes found in restaurants whose standard menus focus on meat. On the other hand, people cook differently at home, following the seasons and family recipes with a focus on vegetables, using fresh ingredients from the garden or preserves from the pantry. This home cuisine has emerged through centuries of observing Lent, which in the Christian Orthodox religion lasts almost 180 days (thankfully not in a row). Also, meat used to be expensive and only for special occasions, while the rest of the time people ate frugally, preparing what they could grow in their gardens or could forage.

In Romania, when it comes to buying good vegetables, we turn to the Bulgarian ethnic communities in the south, in Walachia. They are the most skilful, knowledgeable and hard-working growers we know. They settled here between the 18th and 19th centuries because the life in their homelands ruled by the Ottomans became unbearable, so they crossed the Danube into southern Romania. They brought with them vegetable seeds to secure a source of food and income, and to continue their traditional craft. Legend says that they kept some seeds in their shirts' chest pockets close to their hearts as a symbol of hope for a new beginning.

When the Ottomans noticed the abandoned villages in Bulgaria, they summoned the Walachian prince to send the people back. But the prince valued the newcomers: they worked hard and turned idle land into a productive and flourishing region, so he pretended that the groups were Serbians. The Ottomans couldn't do much but accept the explanation, and since then the Bulgarians in this part of Romania have been known as Serbians, *Sârbi*.

The most famous community is in Băleni-Sârbi, a town an hour away from the capital city, Bucharest, on an old trade route that linked the south to the north of the country. Today, they have thousands of acres of land and polytunnels, making it the largest vegetable-growing area in the country. They have the best tomatoes, herbs, cabbages, runner beans, cucumbers, peppers, horseradish and leaf vegetables, which are sought after in markets across the region and even north in Transylvania.

Orthodox Cuisine

Like Romanians, Bulgarians are Christian Orthodox of the Greek rite, with one exception in the Banat, where we find a few groups of Catholic Bulgarians called Pauliceni. I mention religion at the start of a food conversation because our cuisine is hugely influenced by its fasting–feasting traditions, which have generated a vegan cuisine in the Orthodox rite and a vegetarian cuisine in the Catholic groups. During Lent, Bulgarians love to fill pies with seasonal vegetables mixed with potatoes as a binding ingredient or eat vegetables for breakfast mixed with eggs, like in the recipe on page 36. Pickles and conserves are also popular since people have to preserve the bounty of each season, especially when they grow so many varieties.

To understand Bulgarian cuisine in its motherland, I made a virtual journey across the Danube and talked with Petya Borisova. 'My grandfather, Sredko Milanov Georgiev, was born in a village called Slivata, near Lom in Northern Bulgaria. The village is close to Romania, so he mixed some Romanian words in when he spoke, confusing everyone.' Like many other people from this region, his family owned a large plot of land, producing vegetables for their own needs. Her grandmother, Tsvetanka Metodieva Georgieva, was from southern Bulgaria and met her husband in western Bulgaria, in Pernik. 'So the family dishes were quite varied, but my grandfather didn't like the food in the West, so he cooked from memory the dishes of his childhood.'

Petya remembers stuffed peppers (see a similar recipe on page 158), delicious cabbage with pork or sausages called *varivo* (see a similar recipe on page 204), and slow-cooked bean stew (see page 142), and many recipes with fried or roasted peppers with tomatoes. As she spoke, I found something utterly comforting and familiar in all the dishes we shared on both sides of the Danube river.

Bulgarians use their famous yoghurt and white, brined cheese in pies and dips, and also in a fantastic baked cheese with chopped tomatoes dish (see recipe on page 46). They make a Thracian salad with yoghurt, gherkins, garlic, walnuts and dried dill, and you can read about its many variations on page 29. Of course, there are dishes with meat, such as *kavurma*, made with meat and onions, or *guyveche*, which cooks meat and vegetables in deep clay pots covered with a lid. Shallow ceramic dishes with no lid are called *sach*, donating the name for a whole category of recipes.

Many recipes reflect the Turkish influence, as is often the case in the Balkans, but the land and the knowledge of working it, the produce, and the Bulgarians' distinct character helped the cuisine acquire its own characteristics.

In the true spirit of Bulgarian hospitality, Petya was very generous with her answers, and I could sense the fondness and nostalgia surrounding the dishes we talked about. She lives in Amsterdam, where she cooks Bulgarian dishes for her family and keeps her culinary traditions alive.

HREAN
35 00

Salată Orientală

POTATO AND EGG SALAD WITH OLIVES

When we say 'salad' in Romania, we mean a whole category of dishes made with fresh or cooked ingredients, sliced, diced or mashed. So anything can be a salad, including dips and spreads. We have a long tradition of serving salads as part of the starters, in-between dishes and as side dishes. Historically, salads made up almost a quarter of the menu in inns, urban restaurants and on royal tables. This recipe is one of the most popular potato salads in Romania, and no matter the rest of the ingredients, it needs to have olives. It is an eclectic mix and probably the reason why it is called 'oriental', which is not used in the English sense of China or Asia.

Serves 4

a pinch of salt
500 g (1 lb 2 oz) potatoes,
    unpeeled and cut into
    large cubes
a drizzle of sunflower or olive oil
1 medium red onion, finely sliced
5 medium radishes, finely sliced
¼ cucumber, finely sliced
1 tablespoon chopped fresh dill

For the Dressing

1 tablespoon white wine vinegar
3 tablespoons cold-pressed
    sunflower oil or good olive oil
½ teaspoon salt

To Serve

100 g (3½ oz/¾ cup) pitted
    black olives, halved
4 medium eggs, hard-boiled
    and sliced

Bring a large pan of water to the boil and add a generous pinch of salt. Boil the potatoes until they start to soften – they should be cooked through but still firm. Drain them well, then transfer them to a large bowl. Drizzle a little oil on top to prevent them from drying out.

Mix and toss all the other ingredients together in the bowl with the potatoes.

Make the dressing by whisking all the ingredients together. Pour it over the salad and combine well. Taste and adjust the seasoning, adding more vinegar if needed. Serve warm or cold, with olives on top and slices of boiled egg.

Spanac cu Iaurt si Boia

YOGHURT CREAMED SPINACH WITH PAPRIKA PUMPKIN SEEDS

I found this recipe while researching the Ada Kaleh island on the Danube, which you can read about on page 226. It's called *borani* and can be made with nettles or any other foraged leaves and plants that are full of vitamins in spring. The touch of lively colour comes from *boia,* the name for paprika in southern Romania.

Serves 2

For the Paprika Pumpkin Seed

1 tablespoon sunflower
 or olive oil
35 g (1¼oz) pumpkin seeds
1 pinch of salt
1 teaspoon smoked
 or sweet paprika

For the Spinach

260 g (9½ oz) spinach
25 g (1 oz) unsalted butter
1½ teaspoons plain
 (all-purpose) flour
100 g (3½ oz/generous
 ⅓ cup) yoghurt
60 ml (2 fl oz/¼ cup) water
salt and freshly ground
 black pepper

To Serve

2 fried eggs
buttered toast

Fry the pumpkin seeds in hot oil until they start popping and the skin blisters. Turn the heat to low, add the salt and paprika and cook for a couple more minutes stirring all the time. Transfer onto a plate lined with kitchen towel.

Simmer the spinach for 3 minutes in hot water, transfer it into a sieve, and run it under cold water from the tap. If the spinach is organic or from your garden, you can reserve and drink the blanching water. It contains many vitamins and is very healthy. Squeeze the spinach of as much water as you can and chop it finely.

In a small frying pan (skillet), melt the butter and stir in the flour, cooking on medium heat for 1 minute. Mix in the yoghurt and water, season and cook for another minute until it turns into a thick, smooth sauce. Now stir in the chopped spinach and distribute it evenly in the sauce, cooking on medium heat for 5 minutes, stirring often. Taste and adjust the salt and pepper. Transfer into a shallow bowl, sprinkle the seeds on top and spoon over some paprika oil left in the pan. Serve warm or cold with two fried eggs.

Vinete cu Scordolea

FRIED AUBERGINES WITH GARLIC BREAD SAUCE

A *scordolea* is a bold accompaniment to fish and vegetables, usually made with soaked bread, walnuts or hazelnuts, and a lot of garlic. *Skorda* means 'garlic' in Greek, and their version is made with potatoes. It comes in many variations depending on what is used to thicken the garlic sauce, and is popular not only in Romania but also in the Balkans.

Serves 4

For the Sauce

125 g (4 oz) soft, white, crustless slices of bread
200 ml (7 fl oz/scant 1 cup) full-fat milk, plus extra if needed
100 g (3½ oz/¾ cup) blanched hazelnuts
4 medium garlic cloves
25 ml (scant 2 tablespoons) good sunflower or olive oil, plus extra for drizzling
juice of ½ medium lemon
salt and freshly ground black pepper

For the Aubergines

sunflower oil, for frying
2 medium aubergines (eggplants)
1 tablespoon chopped parsley
salt and freshly ground black pepper

Soak the bread in the milk for 10 minutes.

Use a food processor to grind the hazelnuts to a powder, then add the bread and milk, garlic cloves, a pinch each of salt and pepper, and blend well. Pour in the oil and lemon juice and blend again. Leave it to rest for 5 minutes, then check the consistency. It should be thick enough to barely fall off the spoon, but if you prefer the consistency of hummus, add more milk and blend again. Taste and adjust the seasoning. Set aside.

Heat a thin layer of oil in a large frying pan (skillet) over a medium heat. Cut the aubergines (eggplants) into 1 cm (½ in) round slices and fry for 8 minutes until soft and caramelised around the edges but not mushy. Add a splash more oil, if needed. Season, sprinkle with parsley and serve immediately with the garlic bread sauce, drizzled with a little oil.

Mazăre Frecată

GARDEN PEA SPREAD WITH MINT

This is an incredibly easy dish and I often prepare it instead of white bean dip or hummus. It's refreshing, light and makes your days bright and happy. It can be made with frozen or fresh green peas, skinned baby broad (fava) beans or dried peas, all cooked before blending. It is best left a little coarse. For a non-vegetarian version, top it with slices of grilled sausage or fried lardons and a pinch of paprika.

Serve 4

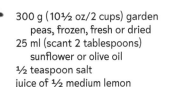

300 g (10½ oz/2 cups) garden peas, frozen, fresh or dried
25 ml (scant 2 tablespoons) sunflower or olive oil
½ teaspoon salt
juice of ½ medium lemon
1 teaspoon freshly chopped mint

To Serve (optional)

sliced bread or toast
radishes, sliced mint leaves, to garnish

If you are using frozen garden peas, put them in a pan of boiling water for a few minutes, then drain and allow to cool. If you are using fresh or dried, you'll have to simmer them gently until cooked, then drain and cool.

   Put the cooked peas in a food processor with the oil, salt and lemon juice, and blend until they reach a spreadable consistency. It doesn't have to be smooth like hummus. Mix in the mint and serve, or refrigerate for 30 minutes to chill. It's very refreshing on slices of toast with radishes, garnished with fresh mint leaves.

The Oltenians

When the Roman Empire conquered the southern lands of today's Romania, including Oltenia, in the 2nd century AD, the region was honoured with the status of province. This lineage had sown the seed for the name that centuries later was to define the whole of the south, Romanian Principality, and then the whole country, Romania.

We think of Oltenians as the direct descendants of those Romans and judge their fiery, passionate temperament as the Latin trait that has remained in their blood since ancient times.

They are also known for their fighting and rebellious spirit, which they might have got from an Asian steppe tribe, the Cumas, who came to the area in the 13th century. Throughout history, from medieval to modern times, Oltenians proved unbreakable and resilient, even stubborn, character traits I know only too well since my grandfather was Oltenian.

The region gets its name from the river Olt, which runs through it, and it is ridged with hills and valleys coming down from the Carpathian mountains. Its vast plain in the south is bordered by the mighty Danube river, upon the far bank of which lies Bulgaria.

It is perhaps this landscape, which often kept the region cut off from neighbouring influences, that has allowed Oltenians to keep their ancestral roots unchanged.

The ancient people of Oltenia cultivated the land with millet, barley and wheat, planted grapevines, and were skilful beekeepers and shepherds. Over the centuries, the region flourished along the trade routes from Transylvania to the Danube and the Black Sea. Its capital, Craiova, gained enough financial and political power to have a special status, Bănia Craiovei, and influenced how the principality was run. Today, it looks eclectic and charming in an old-fashioned Balkan way, and it is here that we discover a connection with the story of Curtișoara, see page 75.

In the kitchen, the most distinctive element of Oltenian cooking is the ash bread baked under *testum*, called țest. This brings the story right back to the beginning and the way the bread was made in Rome and Pompeii (see page 53).

The culinary symbol of Oltenia is the leek, the herbs that flavour the dishes are parsley and lovage, and the sour soups are made with vinegar (the ancient Roman way) or the juice resulting from making sauerkraut. The dishes are a melange of ancient European and Ottoman-influenced Balkan cuisine, including cooking with foraged plants, as in the recipe on page 100.

Păpuși de Dragavei

OLTENIAN ROASTED CHARD WITH GARLIC DRESSING AND CREAMY POLENTA

A clever Oltenian dish, it speaks of seasonality and local knowledge. Traditionally, it is made with dock leaves gathered together in bunches and tied at each end, which we call 'dolls', *păpuși*. The bunches are brushed with oil and thrown onto a hot grill (broiler). While the outside leaves char, the middle stays protected and softens. The result is an exciting contrast of bittersweet, soft and crunchy leaves mellowed by cooking. They are served with soft polenta and drizzled with *mujdei* garlic sauce because Oltenians don't compromise on bold flavours. My recipe is an oven version using chard, but please try it with dock leaves if you can.

Serves 4

For the Garlic Dressing

25 g (1 oz) garlic cloves, sliced
1 teaspoon fine salt
2 tablespoons olive oil
1 tablespoon white wine vinegar
150 ml (5 fl oz/scant ⅔ cup) cold tap water
1 tablespoon chopped basil (optional)

For the Chard

300 g (10½ oz) rainbow chard, whole leaves and stalks
2 tablespoons olive oil
½ teaspoon salt

To Serve

1 batch of *Mămăliga* Polenta (see page 15)

Preheat the oven to 180°C fan (350°F/gas 4).

Make the dressing with a pestle and mortar. Add the garlic and salt, and crush to a smooth paste. Add the olive oil, little by little, and use the pestle in circular movements to blend it in. The consistency should be almost like a mousse. Stir in the vinegar and water, adding the basil at the end (if using). Set aside.

Pat the chard dry, if necessary, and toss in the oil. Place in a single or double layer on a lined baking sheet and sprinkle evenly with the salt. Roast on the lower shelf for 15 minutes until the edges of the leaves are crisp, almost charred, and the middles are soft.

Meanwhile, make the *Mămăligă* Polenta (see page 15). Serve dollops of it topped with chard and spoonfuls of the garlic sauce.

Salată de Ardei Prăjiți

VLACH FRIED PEPPER SALAD

This salad is inspired by the Vlach communities in Romania and Bulgaria, where fried peppers mixed with cheese appear in many dishes. The Vlachs are also called Aromanians and they speak a romance language very similar to Romanian. They live throughout the Balkan countries and north of the Danube in Romania. The recipe makes a good alternative to roasted pepper salad because the method is quicker and fuss-free. The honey and lemon juice mellow the garlic flavour and the dressing has bags of personality.

Serves 4

For the Honey and Garlic Dressing

3 medium garlic cloves, grated
1 teaspoon salt
2 tablespoons olive oil
1 tablespoon juice from
    1 small lemon
4 teaspoons runny honey
25 ml (scant 2 tablespoons)
    water

For the Peppers

2 large Romano peppers
4 teaspoons sunflower
    or vegetable oil

To Serve

50 g (2 oz) white
    or feta-style cheese

For the dressing, use a pestle and mortar to blend the grated garlic and salt with the oil until it emulsifies and thickens. Mix in the lemon juice and honey, then dilute it with water. Set aside.

Slice the peppers into 3–4 cm (1–1½ in) long wedges and scrape off all the seeds. Heat the oil in a frying pan (skillet) over a medium heat and cook the peppers until soft and with lightly burnt patches.

Transfer to a bowl or plate, pour the dressing over and crumble the cheese on top. Allow the flavours to infuse and the dish to cool. Serve with bread or as a side dish.

Drob de Ciuperci

MUSHROOM AND SPRING ONION LOAF

A *drob* is an iconic Easter lamb meatloaf, made with offal and a generous amount of spring onions (scallions), which keep the texture moist. For those who don't like lamb or eat meat, we make a vegetarian version with mushrooms. The boiled eggs are placed inside the loaf or served on the side.

Makes a 900 g (2 lb) loaf

sunflower oil, for frying
500 g (1 lb 2 oz) mushrooms
   (mixed, wild, any type), diced
12 thin spring onions (scallions),
   chopped, including the
   green tops
2 medium garlic cloves, grated
3 medium eggs, beaten
½ tablespoon finely chopped
   fresh dill or fennel or sage
50 g (2 oz/½ cup) fine
   golden breadcrumbs
salt and freshly ground pepper

For the Topping

80 g (3 oz/scant ⅓ cup)
   sour cream or thick yoghurt
15 g (½ oz) salted butter, diced

To Serve (optional)

4 medium eggs, boiled
radishes
mustard

Heat a thin layer of oil in a frying pan (skillet) over a medium heat. Add the mushrooms, onions, garlic and a generous pinch of salt, and cook for 15 minutes until the juices in the pan evaporate. Taste and adjust the seasoning generously. Set aside to cool.

Preheat the oven to 170°C fan (325°F/gas 3). Line a 900 g (2 lb) loaf tin with baking parchment.

Mix the cooled mushroom mixture with the rest of the ingredients. Tip into the loaf tin and press it down lightly, then spread the sour cream evenly on top and dot with the butter. Bake for 45 minutes on a lower shelf.

Remove from the tin onto a plate, allow it to set and cool for 30 minutes, then cover and place it in the refrigerator. Serve cold, with boiled eggs, radishes and small dollops of mustard.

Zacuscă de Pește

FISH AND ROASTED VEGETABLE SPREAD

In northern Dobrogea, along the shores of freshwater lagoons and in the Danube Delta, the cuisine is dominated by fish. This dish is vegetarian on the mainland and pescatarian here, and comes with an intricate story.

In Romania, *zacuscă* is a spread made by slow-cooking different vegetables. It also represents a culinary and linguistic fusion between two elements: vegetable caviar, a mixture made popular by the Ottoman Empire all the way from Persia and India; and the assortment of small plates served with drinks that came from the Swedish courts via Russia, called *zakuski*.

Dr. Cristian Gaşpar, from the Central European University in Vienna, looked into the importance of *zacuscă* in the identity of Romanian cuisine. He found it mentioned at the beginning of the 19th century in commercial ads for tinned fish, usually meaning a mixture of different types of fish, slow-cooked. After WWII, fish being very expensive, it was repurposed as a fried vegetable spread and became the national dish of the post-war food marketing campaign. As we know it today, *zacuscă* is a modern product, although one that has managed to lay perfectly on top of a much older tradition of vegetable caviars that we already had.

Romanians have many variations of the recipe, which incited the publication of a book called *Curatorul de Zacuscă* (The Zacuscă Curator) by Cosmin Dragomir. As he discovered, the roasted pepper base brings the dish into the same Balkan family of the *ajvar*, *lutenita*, *biber salçası* and *pindjur*. From here, the recipe turns into a Romanian adventure by adding any of the following: aubergines (eggplants), tomatoes, mushrooms, white beans, runner beans, garden peas, carrots, courgettes (zucchini), cauliflower, green tomatoes, apples, pears, quince, cinnamon… or fish.

Serves 4

480 g (1 lb 1 oz) salmon fillets
1 large brown onion, sliced
2 red (bell) peppers
generous 2 tablespoons
    sunflower or vegetable oil,
    plus extra for drizzling
2 medium carrots, grated
2 tablespoons tomato purée
    (paste)
200 g (7 oz) chopped tomatoes
4 bay leaves
1 teaspoon juniper berries
½ teaspoon ground cinnamon
1 teaspoon sweet paprika
zest and juice of
    1 medium lemon
salt and freshly ground
    black pepper
thick slices of bread, to serve

Preheat the oven to 180°C fan (350°F/gas 4).

Place the fish fillets together with the slices of onion and peppers on a lined baking sheet, drizzle with oil, sprinkle with a pinch of salt and roast for 15 minutes, or until the fish is cooked and the vegetables start to caramelise around the edges. Remove from the oven and set aside.

Heat the 2 tablespoons of oil in a large frying pan (skillet) over a medium heat. Cook the carrots, stirring often to avoid burning, until they turn a bright, intense orange colour and are soft. Stir in the tomato purée and fry for a couple of minutes. Add the roasted vegetables, chopped tomatoes, bay leaves and spices with ½ teaspoon salt and ¼ teaspoon of pepper. Cook over a medium–low heat for 20 minutes, or until the mixture thickens. Peel off the fish skin, then tear the fish apart in big chunks and add to the stew. Stir in the lemon zest and juice, taste and adjust the seasoning.

Serve warm or cold on thick slices of bread.

Salată de Conopidă

CAULIFLOWER SALAD WITH TOMATO DRESSING

This is a quick way to cook cauliflower without roasting or adding butter or cream. The flavour comes from the fresh and zingy tomato dressing. It can be a side dish served with fish or meat.

Serves 4

1 medium cauliflower
salt
olive oil, to drizzle

For the Dressing

1 medium red onion, finely sliced
½ teaspoon salt
1 tablespoon white wine vinegar
2 large tomatoes (if in season), grated, or 300 g (10 ½ oz/ 1 ¼ cups) tinned chopped tomatoes
1 tablespoon finely chopped parsley

Cut the cauliflower in half from top to bottom, then in half again. Cut the core out and separate the florets. Try to make them all roughly the same size, so cut the larger ones in half. Place them in a deep pan, cover with water, add 1 teaspoon salt and bring to the boil. Cook over a medium–high heat for 12 – 15 minutes until done but not mushy. You can test to see if they are ready by cutting one in half. Drain them in a sieve (fine mesh strainer), then transfer to a bowl and add a generous pinch of salt.

Meanwhile, make the dressing. Mix the red onion with the salt and vinegar, and set aside for 15 minutes. Stir in the chopped tomatoes and parsley, then taste and adjust the seasoning.

Spoon the dressing over the cauliflower and drizzle with a little oil. Serve warm or cold, in which case you can put the bowl in the refrigerator.

Salată de Castraveți

CRÈME FRAÎCHE CUCUMBER AND LETTUCE SALAD

This refreshing salad goes well with any meat or fish dishes. Adding sour cream to fresh, steamed or fried vegetables is a big thing in Romania because it cools you down in the heat of the summer.

Serves 4

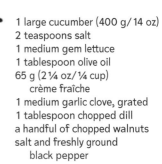

1 large cucumber (400 g/ 14 oz)
2 teaspoons salt
1 medium gem lettuce
1 tablespoon olive oil
65 g (2 ¼ oz/ ¼ cup)
    crème fraîche
1 medium garlic clove, grated
1 tablespoon chopped dill
a handful of chopped walnuts
salt and freshly ground
    black pepper

Slice the cucumber into thin discs, mix with the salt and leave for 15 minutes. Using your hands, squeeze all the moisture out.

Cut the lettuce into ribbons, mix with the cucumber in a bowl and add the olive oil.

Mix the crème fraîche with the garlic and dill, then toss everything together and adjust the seasoning. Sprinkle with the walnuts.

Serve as part of sharing starters or as a side dish to meat and fish.

A LAND

OF
BROTHS

The Intricate World of the Romanian Ciorbă

A Romanian *ciorb*ă or *zeam*ă is a clear soup that has a sour element added at the end of the cooking time. This light acidity transforms it, making the flavours dance together. The soup itself is made with onions, vegetables and herbs, with or without meat or fish. It's our comfort food, restorative and refreshing, that we eat for lunch and dinner, and sometimes even for breakfast.

My mother never bought stock to make soup. When she put the pot on the stove, the home was filled with the sweet aromas of the simmering onions, carrots and parsnips. In Romania, we often make stock like this, covering the vegetables with water and bringing them to a simmer. It makes a mild stock, a poaching liquid that allows the ingredients to remain true to their flavour. Frying them was different, it made a stock able to stand up to beans and pulses in winter. Then, to lift the flavours, the last thing she added was a sharp, sour ingredient.

In southern Romania, especially on our journey along the Danube, the sour element, *acritură*, comes from vinegar. You can also simmer some unripe fruit in the soup, such as mirabelles, damsons, gooseberries or sour plums, and remove them before serving. Or you can use sauerkraut juice or fermented passata (sieved tomatoes), even verjus, which is the juice from unripe grapes.

It is also traditional to add sour cream or crème fraîche mixed with eggs, and even whey, like in a popular fish soup in Dobrogea. We also use *borş*, which is the pale yellow and slightly fizzy juice from fermenting wheat bran and cornmeal. Most of our soups fall into the *ciorbă* or *borş* category, although we have a few called 'sweet', as in without any sour element, and they are not part of this chapter. In the following recipes, I use only those methods that are widely accessible and not time-consuming.

Another element in Romanian soups is the addition of eggs. Beaten eggs are swirled into the broth to make *zdrenţe* (shreds), or whole eggs are poached straight into the soup, the whites absorbing some of the flavours. Even an omelette can be sliced and added at the end.

Finally, but not the least spectacular, is the use of cheese, as you can see in the Vitamin Soup on page 118. Cheese makes the dish more satisfying, adding more flavour, saltiness and texture. My sister's mother-in-law, Carmina, who was an incredible cook, used to add crumbled *telemea* cheese, like feta, to chicken soup with noodles or dumplings. She was from the South, and it's not unusual to find this type of combination there.

In recent years, the culinary conversation in Romania has shifted towards *ciorb*ă or *zeamă* as the national dish. We owe it to Mircea Groza, a food anthropologist, whose work and books have influenced the way we look at this dish. Judging by the incredible diversity of recipes throughout the country, and by the dishes' ubiquity on our tables, Mircea explores the idea that the true spirit of Romanian cuisine lies here. All I can add is: don't be misled by the name *ciorbă*, which is of Turkish origin, as the dish isn't.

Ciorbă de Raci

OLTENIAN STUFFED DRIED PEPPER SOUP

This is a famous soup from Oltenia, with such an intense red colour that it has been nicknamed 'crayfish soup'. In reality, it's a vegetarian dish prepared with dried capia peppers. The peppers thrive in this region and are dried in the hot summer air to be used later in the year. The filling can be rice or a mixture of onions and flour, which is delicious.

Serves 4-6

Place the dried peppers in a large bowl and cover them generously with hot water.

For the filling, heat a thin layer of sunflower oil in a 28 cm (11 in) frying pan (skillet) over a medium heat. Add the onions and a good pinch of salt, coat them well in the oil and cook for 20 minutes. Keep stirring so they don't burn. Sprinkle the flour on top, combine well and cook for a further 5 minutes. Stir in the rest of the ingredients and cook the mixture until it reaches the consistency of a very thick paste, around 8 minutes. It will start catching on the pan's bottom, so stir often. When it is ready, taste and adjust the seasoning, and set it aside to cool.

For the soup, heat a thin layer of sunflower oil in a 22 cm (8½ in) deep stock pan over a medium heat. Add the onion, carrots and parsnip with a good pinch of salt and sauté until they begin to caramelise. Pour over the stock together with the passata and bring to a gentle simmer. Keep it on a low heat while you prepare the peppers.

Drain the peppers and carefully fill them three-quarters full with the filling mixture. Use a teaspoon or your index finger to push the filling down away from the rim of the peppers. Place them in the soup broth, add the lemon juice or vinegar and bring the heat up for a few minutes, then readjust to a gentle simmer so that the filling doesn't escape the peppers. Cook for 30 minutes until the peppers are soft. Taste the soup and add more salt if needed.

Serve hot with the parsley sprinkled on top with thick slices of bread, such as the Yeasted Horseradish Cornbread (*Mălai Copt cu Hrean*, page 73) or the Oltenian Ash Bread (*Pâine la Țest*, page 53).

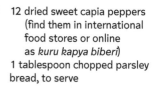

12 dried sweet capia peppers (find them in international food stores or online as *kuru kapya biberi*)
1 tablespoon chopped parsley
bread, to serve

For the Filling

sunflower oil, for frying
500 g (1 lb 2 oz) brown onions, finely sliced
a pinch of salt, or as needed
50 g (2 oz/scant ½ cup) plain (all-purpose) flour
juice of 1 large lemon
1 tablespoon white wine vinegar
80 ml (2½ fl oz/5 tablespoons) passata (sieved tomatoes)

For the Soup

sunflower oil, for frying
1 medium brown onion, finely sliced
2 medium carrots, grated
1 medium parsnip, grated
a pinch of salt, or as needed
1 litre (34 fl oz/4½ cups) vegetable stock
100 ml (3½ fl oz/scant ½ cup) passata (sieved tomatoes)
juice of 1 large lemon or 1 tablespoon white wine vinegar

Note

These peppers also grow south of the Danube, in Bulgaria and Serbia, and further down in Turkey. In Bulgaria, they can also be filled with cooked heirloom dried beans and served on a platter without any sauce, sometimes next to stuffed vine leaves and other vegetables. In Serbia,

the peppers are filled with rice and cooked in a thick tomato sauce. All of these dishes are part of a large family of dried vegetables stuffed with meat or rice and popularised by the Ottomans who ruled these parts of the Balkans and Europe for centuries.

Ciorbă de Cuie

VITAMIN SOUP WITH SPRING ONIONS, LETTUCE AND EGGS

A recipe from the Danube Gorges, it is nicknamed the iron or vitamin soup because it combines all the fortifying goodness of spring and summer produce: lettuce, spring onions (scallions) and spring garlic, herbs, fermented dairy and eggs. I learned to make it in Sviniţa from Lina Dragotoiu, a remarkable woman proud of her Serbian dishes in this part of Romania.

Serves 4

sunflower oil, for frying
30 thin spring onions (scallions) (around 4 standard store-bought bunches), green tops included, sliced
5 medium garlic cloves (or 5 spring garlic/garlic greens, which is similar to spring onions (scallions), green tops included), sliced
1 litre (34 fl oz/4½ cups) vegetable stock
1 romaine lettuce, sliced
20 g (¾ oz) dill, finely chopped, plus extra to garnish
20 g (¾ oz) parsley, chopped
4 medium eggs (1 per person)
200 g (7 oz) *brânză telemea* or Lancashire cheese, crumbled
salt and freshly ground black pepper
a handful of chives, chopped, to garnish

For the Dressing

50 g (2 oz/scant ¼ cup) sour cream
1 medium egg

Heat a thin layer of oil on the base of a deep soup or casserole pan. Fry the onions and garlic over a medium heat with a few pinches of salt for 5 minutes, then add the stock. Bring to the boil, add the lettuce and herbs, cover the pan and simmer gently for another 5 minutes.

Meanwhile, mix the sour cream with the egg for the dressing and set aside.

You will have time to poach the eggs. My host would just crack the eggs straight into the soup, the whites absorbing some of the flavours. I prefer to do this separately. Boil some water in a smaller pan, enough to submerge the eggs. Turn the heat to low, then gently crack in the eggs. Work with one or two at a time. Poach for 2–3 minutes until the whites look opaque and the eggs are springy to the touch. Transfer to a plate greased with a little oil and repeat with the rest.

Take the soup off the heat and stir in the cheese. Cover and leave for a few minutes, then add the sour cream dressing and stir quickly. Taste and adjust the seasoning. Gently slide the poached eggs into the soup to warm and infuse them. Serve with extra dill and chopped chives.

Ciorbă de Legume

WALACHIAN SOUR VEGETABLE SOUP

This is a classic Romanian *ciorbă* that can be made with any vegetables in season. As discussed on page 115, the recipe uses a sour ingredient added towards the end that not only gives the soup a new flavour dimension but also makes it refreshing. Parsley, lovage or celery leaves flavour the broth while cooking, rather than just being used for decoration. As with most *ciorbe* in the south, they are left 'clear' without any further addition of sour cream and eggs.

This is a family recipe that both my mum and grandmother made often and served with croutons or toast. It is a glorious celebration of vegetables, flavour and simplicity.

Serves 4

sunflower oil, for frying
2 medium brown onions,
    finely sliced
1 medium carrot, diced
1 medium parsnip, diced
2 celery stalks, diced
2 pinches of salt
400 g (14 oz) tinned
    chopped tomatoes
1 tablespoon chopped lovage
    or parsley, plus extra to serve
1 litre (34 fl oz/4½ cups) good
    vegetable stock
1 medium red (bell) pepper, diced
2 medium potatoes, cut into
    2–3 cm (¾–1 in) cubes
1 small cauliflower, cut into
    2–3 cm (¾–1 in) pieces
1 small courgette (zucchini),
    grated
4 teaspoons white wine vinegar

To Serve (optional)

pickled chillies
toast

Heat a thin layer of oil on the base of a soup or deep casserole pan over a medium heat. Fry the onions, carrot, parsnip and celery together with a couple of pinches of salt for 15 minutes, stirring occasionally to avoid burning. Add the chopped tomatoes and lovage or parsley, and bring to the boil. Pour in the stock and add the rest of the ingredients apart from the courgette and vinegar. Bring to the boil, cover the pan and simmer for 20 minutes until the potatoes and cauliflower are cooked but not mushy.

Mix in the grated courgette and vinegar, cover the pan and turn off the heat. Leave for another 5 minutes, then serve. Pickled chillies go well with the dish also.

Borş Pescăresc

FISHERMAN'S SOUP

This is the culinary symbol of the entire Danube Delta and the dish everyone eats when holidaying in this part of Dobrogea. Its story begins with a way of life: fishermen out on the lagoons or river canals make a very quick soup to use up any fish they don't sell at a *cherhana*, a fish sorting point. They add something sour, usually vinegar, which firms up the fish flesh and intensifies the flavour. At home, it is mostly prepared by women, who add more flavourings, such as vegetables and herbs, something not available to the men out on a boat, unless they use foraged plants.

For centuries, fishing in the Delta has been associated with the villages of Zaporozhian Cossacks and Russian Old Believers. They are two north Slavic groups who settled in Dobrogea fleeing their lands in today's Ukraine and Russia. Their common Slavic background and skills as fishermen also meant they shared a particular knowledge in fish preparation and preservation.

A fish *borş* is made with different types of fish, the more the better, which together with different vegetables develop a flavoursome stock. It is served in the traditional way, by removing the cooked fish onto a platter next to a side dish of crème fraîche, *smântână*, mixed with garlic. The soup is served on its own as a separate course.

In this recipe I offer a more practical alternative made with one type of fish, traditional to the Delta and also available online: catfish. It is the best option I could offer you for a dish that tastes as close as possible to the original. Alternatively, you can use tilapia or haddock loins. Ready-made fish stock is another shortcut, to replace the lack of different types of fish.

The result is an exquisite soup that will make you travel to the Delta as soon as you taste it. You will return year after year.

Serves 4

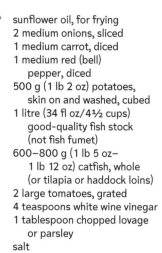

sunflower oil, for frying
2 medium onions, sliced
1 medium carrot, diced
1 medium red (bell)
  pepper, diced
500 g (1 lb 2 oz) potatoes,
  skin on and washed, cubed
1 litre (34 fl oz/4½ cups)
  good-quality fish stock
  (not fish fumet)
600–800 g (1 lb 5 oz–
  1 lb 12 oz) catfish, whole
  (or tilapia or haddock loins)
2 large tomatoes, grated
4 teaspoons white wine vinegar
1 tablespoon chopped lovage
  or parsley
salt

To Serve

150 g (5 oz/scant ⅔ cup)
  crème fraîche
2 medium garlic cloves, grated
a pinch of salt

Heat a thin layer of oil on the base of a soup pan or deep casserole dish over a medium heat and cook the onions with the carrot and a pinch of salt until they start to soften and caramelise. Stir in the peppers and cook for a few more minutes, then add the potatoes and combine well. Pour over the stock and simmer until the potatoes are cooked.

Meanwhile, cut the fish into 5–6 segments, including the tail and the head (the latter is optional, you can discard it). If you are using loins, there is no need to slice them. Add the grated tomatoes

and vinegar to the soup, then gently place the fish in the pan. Simmer over a low heat for 15 minutes if you are using catfish. For tilapia or haddock, 5 minutes is enough. Taste and adjust the seasoning. Turn off the heat and add the lovage or parsley.

Combine the crème fraîche with the garlic and a pinch of salt. You can serve the dish the traditional way described in the introduction or as one dish adding the crème fraîche mixture to the soup before taking it off the heat.

Ciorbă de Perișoare de Pește cu Izmă

SOUP WITH FISH DUMPLINGS AND MINT

A *perișoară* is a dumpling made with meat, fish or vegetables. The most famous Romanian dumpling soup is made with minced (ground) pork, but here I have a river version with fish. Mint, especially spearmint, has a wonderful sweetness, which makes it perfect for pairing with delicate ingredients like fish.

Serves 4 (makes 12 fish dumplings)

For the Dumplings

350 g (12 oz) skinless cod fillet, fresh or frozen
1 medium garlic clove
1 teaspoon salt
200 g (7 oz/1 generous cup) cooked plain rice
1 small egg
1 tablespoon finely chopped fresh spearmint or mint

For the Soup

sunflower oil, for frying
1 medium brown onion, sliced
1 medium fennel bulb, sliced
400 g (14 oz) tinned plum tomatoes
1 litre (34 fl oz/4½ cups) fish stock (if you use fumet, skip the tomatoes)
juice of 1 medium lemon
1 tablespoon chopped fresh herbs, such as fennel, parsley, lovage or a mix of all, to serve

If you are using frozen fish, thaw it first, then pat it dry with paper towel. Place the fish in a food processor with the garlic and salt, and blend to a paste. Add the rice, egg and mint, blending them briefly. Cover and refrigerate until you are ready to shape the dumplings.

Heat a little oil in a 20 cm (8 in) pan that has a lid over a medium heat. Add the onions and cook until they start to soften, then add the fennel and cook for a further 5 minutes. Chop the plum tomatoes roughly and add to the pan together with their sauce, bringing to the boil. Stir in the fish stock and lemon juice, and when everything starts to bubble vigorously, turn the heat to low.

Shape twelve 45 g (1¾ oz) dumplings from the fish mixture and gently drop them into the stock. I use my hands to roll them into balls, but you can use a spoon to make them slightly elongated. Cover the pan and simmer very gently for 20 minutes. Adjust the heat so the liquid stays almost still. The dumplings are very delicate, especially at the beginning, but they will firm up during cooking.

Serve immediately with a sprinkle of mixed herbs.

Lacșa

TATAR SOUP WITH BEANS AND WIDE NOODLES

Noodles are an important part of Tatar cooking and the base for varied combinations with seasonal vegetables and legumes. The white beans are good for texture since they are slightly firmer, and also for adding more protein to a meal without using meat. It's a silky-smooth and practical dish, a favourite of many Tatars who mentioned it in conversations about comfort food, family memories, and what to cook for children when they come back from school.

Serves 4

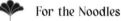

For the Noodles

200 g (7 oz/1⅔ cups) plain
    (all-purpose) flour,
    plus extra for dusting
2 medium eggs
a splash of water, if needed
a pinch of salt
OR
200 g (7 oz) tagliatelle

For the Dressing

150 g (5 oz/scant ⅔ cup)
    full-fat plain yoghurt
4 medium garlic cloves, grated,
    plus extra to serve (if wished)

For the Soup

1.5 litres (51 fl oz/6 cups)
    vegetable stock
600 g (1 lb 5 oz) white beans
    from a jar
a drizzle of olive oil, to serve

If making your own noodles, knead all the ingredients together until smooth and elastic. Cover and leave to rest for 15 minutes, then divide the dough in half and roll each piece as thinly as possible. Place the dough on a cloth dish towel away from the steam in the kitchen and allow it to dry for 30 minutes. Sprinkle generously with flour, then roll it up and slice across the roll into 3 mm (⅛ in) strips. Alternatively, you can use a pasta machine and the tagliatelle setting or store-bought pasta. Sprinkle the cut noodles with flour and put your fingers through them to separate the curls and fluff up.

Meanwhile, make the dressing by combining the yoghurt and garlic. Set aside.

Bring the stock for the soup to the boil, then add the pasta and beans. Cook for 3–5 minutes until the pasta is done but still firm. Take off the heat and add some of the broth to the yoghurt mixture, combining it well, then pour it into the soup. Stir to distribute the mixture evenly.

Serve with a drizzle of oil and more grated garlic, if needed.

Curban

LAMB SOUP WITH PEARL BARLEY AND MINT

The name *Curban* may sound familiar to those who know about the Muslim festival called *Kurban Bayram*, the Feast of the Sacrifice. Although the Ottomans spread the name to the Balkans, the tradition is a social practice that holds cultural significance across many religions, including Christianity. It is a powerful way for people to come together around a dish that is both life-giving and healing.

In Romania, the Greek villages in the south celebrate *Curban* publicly on St. George's Day, the patron of shepherds. The purpose is to appease fate and secure prosperity in the new farming year. *Curban* is traditionally associated with a patrilineal hierarchy, so the sacrificed animal must be a male, usually a lamb, the same as at Easter. However, there are variations for less-special occasions with cockerels, ganders, or rams. Before roasting, the *Curban* is purified by sprinkling salt and smoking it with frankincense. It is then basted while cooking with bunches of basil, spearmint or rosemary, symbols of new life and regeneration. The whole community must share the roast together and once finished, the bones are buried in the ground to ensure good fortune for all.

The rituals take many forms throughout the Muslim and Christian world, from public celebrations to private rituals for health. In Bulgaria, south of the Danube, it is celebrated on both *Sabor*, the Saint day of the family, and as a thank you on a meaningful day when one surmounted a difficult challenge. The lamb dish is a soup, not a roast, and is the version that follows in the recipe opposite.

Serves 4–6

1.5 litres (51 fl oz/6 cups) lamb or beef stock
1.2 kg (2 lb 11 oz) lamb shank (2–3 pieces)
1 medium leek, sliced, including the green tops
2 teaspoons dried spearmint or mint, plus extra to serve
2 medium carrots, cut into 2 cm (¾ in) chunks
2 medium parsnips, cut into 2 cm (¾ in) chunks
2 medium red (bell) peppers, sliced
180 g (6 oz/generous ¾ cup) pearl barley
salt and freshly ground black pepper

In a large pan with a lid, bring the stock and the lamb shanks to the boil. Reduce the heat to medium–low to simmer gently and add the leeks and dried mint. Cover the pan and cook for 1 hour 20 minutes, checking occasionally to see that it's not boiling too fast or too slow, then adjust the heat.

Add the carrots, parsnips, peppers and pearl barley, cover and cook for another 45 minutes.

By this time, the meat should be tender and falling off the bone. Take the pan off the heat and remove the shanks from the soup. When they are cool enough to touch, discard the bones and portion the meat into large chunks. Return the meat to the pan and reheat, then taste and adjust the seasoning. Cover and cook for 5 minutes.

Serve immediately, sprinkled with more mint.

Ciorbă de Văcuță

BEEF AND VEGETABLE SOUP

Travel to any corner of Romania and you will find this *ciorbă* in all restaurants and bistros. It is made with diced beef and vegetables, and soured with vinegar, as with many *ciorbe* served in the south. The tanginess makes it perfect for summer days when it's very refreshing.

Serves 4

sunflower oil, for frying
500 g (1 lb 2 oz) diced beef shin
2 medium onions, diced
1 medium carrot, diced
1 medium parsnip, diced
1 celery stalk, sliced
scant 2 tablespoons tomato
    purée (paste)
1 litre (34 fl oz/4½ cups)
    good-quality beef stock
1 tablespoon finely chopped
    parsley, plus extra to serve
200 g (7 oz) French beans,
    trimmed and cut into 3 cm
    (1 in) pieces
200 g (7 oz) garden peas, fresh
    or frozen
80 ml (2½ fl oz/5 tablespoons)
    white wine vinegar
salt and freshly ground
    black pepper

Heat a thin layer of oil on the base of a large deep soup pan or casserole dish with a lid over a medium heat.

Brown the meat well, then remove it to a plate and set aside.

Add just enough oil to the pan to cover the base again and cook the onions, carrot, parsnip and celery with a pinch of salt for 15 minutes over a medium heat. Stir often and allow the vegetables to caramelise slightly. Stir in the tomato purée, combine well and cook for a couple more minutes. Return the beef to the pan, pour the stock in, add the parsley and bring to the boil. Reduce the heat, cover the pan and simmer gently for 1 hour 10 minutes, or until the beef is tender.

Taste and adjust the salt and pepper. Add the French beans and garden peas, and cook until the beans are done. Mix in the vinegar and simmer for 5 more minutes, then taste to see if it needs more. I like this soup to be quite tangy, but it's a matter of personal preference. Turn the heat off and leave covered for another 5 minutes before serving.

Sprinkle with the extra parsley and serve it with more vinegar on the side for people to flavour it to their liking.

Supă de Roșii cu Găluște

TOMATO SOUP WITH CHEESE SEMOLINA DUMPLINGS

This was one of my favourite soups when I was little. It is a good combination of the satisfying smoothness of dumplings with the sweet and tangy flavours of tomatoes.

Serves 4

For the Soup

125 g (4 oz) sundried tomatoes
scant 2 tablespoons tomato purée (paste)
1½ teaspoons white wine vinegar
500 ml (17 fl oz/2 cups) passata (sieved tomatoes)
400 ml (13 fl oz/generous 1½ cups) water
1 organic vegetable stock cube
salt and freshly ground black pepper, to taste

For the Dumplings

75 g (2½ oz) salted butter, softened
2 medium eggs
120 g (4 oz/1 cup) semolina
65 g (2¼ oz) Romanian *cașcaval* or Cheddar, grated, plus extra to serve
a pinch each of salt and freshly ground black pepper

Use a food processor to blend the sundried tomatoes with some of the oil from the jar, or carefully chop them by hand. Fry them in a soup pan for 3–4 minutes, then stir in the tomato purée and cook for another 2 minutes. Add the vinegar and allow it to evaporate, then add the rest of the soup ingredients. Cook over a low heat for 25 minutes.

Bring a separate pan of water to the boil. Prepare the dumplings by beating the butter until fluffy, then add the eggs and incorporate well. Mix in the rest of the dumpling ingredients. Use a soup spoon (or two if you want to make quenelles) to drop some batter into the hot water. Don't fill the spoon with the mixture, use just over half of what it can hold. Turn the heat to low and gently simmer the dumplings for 12–15 minutes until doubled in size and fluffy. Test one to see if they are done, then remove with a slotted spoon to the soup pan. Work in batches if necessary, dropping the dumplings into the soup when ready.

Serve immediately with more grated cheese on top.

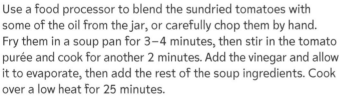

A LAND

OF
VEGETABLES

A Land of Vegetables

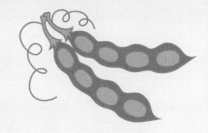

In this chapter, you will find recipes for vegetarian main courses from a runner bean stew and garden peas with eggy bread, to a fantastic potato dish with cheese filo crust and noodles with sauerkraut. It is also the chapter where, in our long journey following the Danube through its Eastern lands, we have reached Dobrogea.

Dobrogea

Dobrogea lies in southern Romania and is the last land the Danube river runs through before flowing into the Black Sea. A legend says that the Argonauts stopped here on their way back from Colchis, having found the Golden Fleece. In people's hearts, it is the cradle of our Christian faith, harbouring some of its first historical traces in Europe. Its mountains are so old, and their peaks so weathered that they now resemble hills and plateaus. The ancient caves, canyons and the northernmost subtropical forest on the continent, Letea, have been inhabited since the 6th millennium BC.

The origin of the name Dobrogea is still disputed. It can mean 'the good land', since the grass and shrublands of the Eurasian steppe descended into the marshy, fertile lands of the Danube Delta. Then I found it meant 'rocky barren land', which I thought was more suited for inland Dobrogea, prone to drought and away from the river with its nourishing fresh waters.

The Land of the Danube Delta, Northern Dobrogea

The Danube splits into three river arms in Tulcea, the landmark city of northern Dobrogea. Chilia is in the north, reaching the border with Ukraine and following it into the Black Sea. The middle channel, Sulina, is the shortest and was rendered navigable in the late-19th century by three British engineers: Sir John Stokes, Sir Charles Hartley and Charles Kuhl, appointed by the European Commission of the Danube. The third, Sf. Gheorghe is the oldest and named after St. George, its serpentine flow evocative of the dragon the saint defeated. This channel sees the least river traffic of the three, hence is the wildest and best for exploring the natural wonders of the entire delta, which is known as the 'European Amazon'. There is a fourth canal, this time in southern Dobrogea, which was completely man-made for commercial purposes, connecting the Black Sea with the Danube on the shortest route possible from the maritime port Constanța. It was constructed by convicts, especially political prisoners and dissidents who opposed the Communist regime, and they had to dig it up by hand in horrible conditions. Two hundred thousand people died here between 1976 and 1987, and with them an entire social middle and upper class was dismantled.

The Land of the Black Sea, Southern Dobrogea

In the south, Dobrogea is dominated by the Black Sea, following its shores into the neighbouring Balkans. As a historic region, it belongs to Romania and Bulgaria and has seen many changes in fate. Here, Constanța is its capital, formerly named Tomis by the ancient Greeks and Romans. The latter even sent their most beloved author, Ovidius, into exile here as the furthest, wildest outpost of the Roman empire. It was renamed Constantia in the Byzantine age, after the sister of the Emperor Constantine the Great. To this day, the city has remained one of the most ethnically rich places in Romania, with a Balkan feel in the Old Town and its narrow streets dotted with stylish European buildings of the 19th and 20th centuries.

A Welcoming Land

For millennia, this land has seen layer upon layer of settlers and rulers. From the Dacian and Gatae tribes to the Greek colonies and the Roman Empire, the settlements were turned into cultural 'melting pots' and commercial hubs. The region became one of the empire's most Romanised, fortified and long-lived Roman frontiers, with vestiges and effects visible even today. Tatar and Ottoman waves swept through Europe, but their presence in Dobrogea was mostly military and didn't disturb commerce and the arrangements of everyday life. Anybody was welcome in these borderlands, and many came here searching for sanctuary, fleeing their own countries. Today, to be a Romanian in Dobrogea means to have many ethnic veins running through your ancestry: Greek, Tatar, Turkish, Vlach Aromanian, Armenian, Roma-Gypsy, Russian, Cossack, Circassian, Bulgarian, German, Gagauz and Italian. 'The key words in our region are tolerance and harmony,' said Alexandru Chiselev, one of the most respected historians of Dobrogean ethnic diversity. And it is what I've seen.

In the Kitchen

The cuisine is as diverse as the people of Dobrogea. From the Danube Delta to the Black Sea, coastal cuisine is dominated by fish, while inland it is about shepherds and millers, vegetable growers and farmers. Archaeological discoveries found traces of wheat and millet, lentils and pearl barley, grape seeds and Cornelian cherries, and also dairy, possibly from the aurochs grazing these steppe lands. These ingredients have remained in the region's culinary DNA, and you will find them throughout this book (less the auroch milk, of course).

Dobrogea was renowned for the strong winds that blew incessantly, whose power was harnessed by windmills. Until the 20th century, hundreds of wooden windmills were dotted across the region, much like a Dutch landscape, and today would have attracted thousands of tourists had they not been demolished in the name of modernisation. Not a single one has survived.

Millers produced the very good quality flour needed for making filo pastry, which is the most popular element in a large variety of pies and pastries. The tradition has given us the famous recipe of the region: *Plăcintă Dobrogeană*, savoury cheese pie (see page 60).

Meat was for special occasions, with lamb, mutton or beef more likely to appear in Turkish and Tatar dishes, while pork in Romanian, Greek and Armenian. People cooked with foraged plants, especially the Vlachs, Aromanians and Macedonians, famous for their plant-filled pies. Rice and potatoes might be a staple today, as in many parts of the world, but orzo, burghul wheat and noodles were more important in many Dobrogean dishes in the past.

Mâncare de Fasole Verde

RUNNER BEAN STEW

We love runner beans in Romania. For those of us who are keen gardeners, they are also very rewarding to grow. One of the best ways to prepare them to feed a family quickly is this summer stew, using a handful of ingredients. I always serve it with thick slices of bread, which take the dish to another level.

Serves 4

sunflower oil, for frying
2 medium brown onions, chopped
2 large ripe tomatoes, chopped, or 200 g (7 oz) tinned chopped tomatoes
500 g (1 lb 2 oz) runner beans, topped and tailed, cut into 2–3 cm (¾–1 in) segments
500 ml (17 fl oz/2 cups) vegetable stock
15 g (½ oz/2 tablespoons) plain (all-purpose) flour
1 tablespoon water
3 medium garlic cloves, grated
20 g (¾ oz) parsley, chopped, plus extra to garnish
salt and freshly ground black pepper
sour cream and bread, to serve (optional)

Heat a thin layer of oil on the base of a 24 cm (9½ in) sauté pan over a medium heat and cook the onions with a good pinch of salt for 12 minutes until soft and translucent. Add the chopped tomatoes, runner beans and vegetable stock, and bring to the boil. Taste to adjust the saltiness. Cover the pan and cook over a medium heat until soft but still retaining their crunch, around 8 minutes.

Meanwhile, put the flour in a mug and combine it with the water little by little to form a paste. When the beans are ready, stir the flour paste into the sauce, add the garlic and parsley, and combine well. Cook for another 2 minutes, then turn the heat off and allow the stew to sit for another 2 minutes before serving.

Divide among bowls, season to taste and scatter with extra parsley. I often add a dollop of sour cream, which is more of a thing in Moldavia than along the banks of the Danube.

Ciulama de Ciuperci

MUSHROOMS IN SOUR CREAM SAUCE WITH POLENTA

I'm always looking forward to this dish for its wonderful, almost custard-like sauce. A *ciulama* is a dish from southern Romania, a white sauce usually made with flour fried in butter, to which we add garlic as the main flavouring, stock, then mushrooms or chicken. Older recipes also contain broad (fava) beans, and surprisingly a sauce made with sour cream that avoids frying flour. This is what I do in the recipe below. *Ciulama* is always served with *mămăligă* (polenta) to bring the flavours together.

Serves 4

400 g (14 oz) white baby
    button mushrooms
1 medium brown onion, sliced
30 g (1 oz/¼ cup) plain
    (all-purpose) flour
120 g (4 oz/½ cup) sour cream
4 medium garlic cloves, grated
½ teaspoon fine salt, or to taste
10 g (½ oz) parsley, chopped
a knob of unsalted butter, diced

To Serve

1 batch of *Mămăligă* Polenta
    (see page 15)

Place the mushrooms and onion in a medium pan and cover with water. Simmer gently for 10–12 minutes until the mushrooms start to soften.

Meanwhile, mix the flour with the sour cream, garlic and salt. Start making the polenta and keep it on a low heat.

When the mushrooms are cooked, discard some of the water, leaving the mushrooms only half or even a little less submerged. Stir in the sour cream mixture and cook over a medium heat for a couple of minutes to allow the flour to thicken. It needs to have the consistency of single (light) cream. Taste and season if necessary. Cover with a lid or a large plate and keep the pan on a low heat while you are finishing the polenta.

Serve the *ciulama* with the polenta, with small dots of butter on top and some chopped parsley.

Iahnie de Fasole cu Scovergi

BEAN STEW WITH CHEESE FLATBREADS AND PICKLED ONIONS

Iahnie is a way of cooking with just enough liquid for the ingredients to infuse and melt together. It's a Persian technique brought to the Balkans and north of the Danube by the Ottomans, who used it in meat dishes with beans, pulses and vegetables. In Romania, it is almost always a white bean stew without meat, although I found old recipes that used potatoes, peas and even octopus instead. I serve my *iahnie* with *scovergi*, fried cheese flatbreads with crispy edges and a gooey middle, for a more satisfying meal.

Serves 4

Start by mixing together all the ingredients for the flatbreads, except for the cheese and oil. Knead until smooth, cover and leave in a warm place for 30 minutes. It should be a sticky dough, so add a splash of water if it looks too dry after mixing. A soft dough will make the breads light. Mix the cheese into the dough and leave it to prove for another 30 minutes.

Make the pickled onions by mixing the ingredients and rubbing the salt into the onion slices. Set aside.

Meanwhile, heat a thin layer of oil on the base of a large sauté pan with a lid over a medium heat. Cook the onions and carrots for 10 minutes until they start to caramelise. Add a splash of water to avoid burning. Stir in the garlic, cook for a further 2 minutes, then add the rest of the ingredients, apart from the tarragon. Cover the pan, reduce the heat to low and cook for 30 minutes, stirring occasionally so the beans don't catch on the bottom of the pan. Add the tarragon before serving.

In the last 10 minutes, divide the bread dough into 4 equal parts and roll each out to a 16 cm (6¼ in) circle. Flour your work surface and rolling pin, if necessary.

Heat a generous layer of oil in a frying pan (skillet) over a medium heat and fry each bread for 3 minutes, turning often. I like to fry one at a time, so I can use a small pan and also not too much oil. Keep the breads on a plate wrapped in kitchen foil while you cook the rest.

Serve immediately with the bean stew and pickled onions.

For the Cheese Flatbreads

225 g (8 oz/1¾ cups) strong bread flour, plus extra for dusting
3 g (½ teaspoon) fine salt
3 g (¾ teaspoon) caster (superfine) sugar
5 g (¾ sachet) fast-action dried yeast
1 tablespoon sunflower or olive oil
120 ml (4 fl oz/½ cup) water
50 g (2 oz) Romanian *cașcaval* cheese or Cheddar, grated
sunflower oil, for frying

For the Pickled Onions

1 medium red onion, sliced
1 tablespoon white wine vinegar
½ teaspoon salt

For the Bean Stew

sunflower oil, for frying
2 large brown onions, sliced
2 medium carrots, sliced
4 medium garlic cloves, sliced
4 teaspoons tomato purée (paste)
400 g (14 oz) cooked white haricot beans from a jar or tin
400 g (14 oz) tinned finely chopped tomatoes
4 teaspoons white wine vinegar
1 teaspoon caster (superfine) sugar
3 bay leaves
1 tablespoon chopped tarragon, dill or parsley

Mâncare de Praz cu Măsline

LEEK STEW WITH OLIVES

All dishes with leeks have dual nationality in my family. My grandfather, Gheorghe, was from Oltenia, where leeks are considered a culinary symbol, and I now live in Wales, UK, where they play a similar role. What a coincidence. This stew is very popular, especially during Lent (skipping the wine) and I love it for its sweet-tangy notes and how quickly it comes together. It is usually served with bread, but I've heard that burghul wheat and rice are also common south of the Danube.

Serves 4

sunflower oil, for frying
2 large leeks, washed and
    cut into round slices,
    green tops included
1 teaspoon coriander seeds
50 ml (1¾ fl oz/3 tablespoons)
    white wine
200 ml (7 fl oz/scant 1 cup)
    vegetable stock
2 x 400 g (14 oz) tins
    of chopped tomatoes
250 g (9 oz) mixed olives,
    plain or marinated
zest and juice of 2 lemons
salt and freshly ground
    black pepper

Cover the base of a large frying pan (skillet) with a thin layer of oil and heat well. Add the sliced leeks with a pinch of salt and the coriander seeds, and cook over a medium heat until well caramelised. Pour in the wine and allow it to evaporate, then add the stock and the chopped tomatoes, and cook for 15 minutes on a low–medium heat. You can cover the pan with a lid, in which case you need to reduce the heat even more to a gentle bubble.

Add the olives, lemon zest and juice, and cook for 5 minutes more. Adjust the seasoning to taste.

Serve with bread, burghul wheat or rice.

Gutui cu Orez

QUINCE AND RICE WITH ROSEMARY

This is one of my favourite dishes when I observe Lent, and it was prepared very often in my family when quinces were in season. Outside Lent, we add chicken or beef. It is a wonderfully perfumed stew with a touch of spiciness from the rosemary. Some recipes go heavy on the savoury caramel sauce, bringing it closer to its ancient Persian origins.

Serves 4

3 medium quince (around 500 g/
   1 lb 2 oz prepared weight)
30 g (1 oz) unsalted butter
2 teaspoons caster
   (superfine) sugar
100 g (3½ oz/½ cup)
   long-grain rice
4 teaspoons dark rum
   (or fruit brandy)
500 ml (17 fl oz/2 cups)
   vegetable stock
4 thin rosemary sprigs

Preheat the oven to 180°C fan (350°F/gas 4).

Quarter the quince, remove the core, trim the ends, then halve the slices again.

Melt the butter in a deep, ovenproof 25cm (10 in) frying pan (skillet). Cook the quince slices in one layer for 5 minutes over a medium–low heat, sprinkling the sugar over halfway through. Turn often so the slices caramelise slightly on both sides. If you need to cook them in two batches, add more butter each time and divide the sugar between them.

Add the rice to the quince and combine well. Turn the heat up for 10 seconds, then pour over the rum, shake the pan, and cook for about 1 minute. Add the stock and rosemary, stirring carefully so all the ingredients are combined well. Transfer the pan uncovered to the oven and cook for 25 minutes on a lower shelf.

Serve immediately.

Păturată pe Crumpi

POTATO STEW WITH CHEESE FILO CRUST

This magnificent dish from Banat combines our Balkan spirit with our traditional Swabian cuisine. *Păturată* means 'blanket', in this case made of filo, and *crumpi* means 'potatoes'. Initially, it was a dish of poverty when the pastry was used to cover the pot and keep the potatoes cooking in their own steam. It has evolved with the wealth of the households and turned into a cheese-filled strudel, swirled to the size of the pan and placed on top of the potatoes. Covered with a lid, the pan was put in the oven.

My recipe is an easier version, a little fiddly to start with but rewarding. Most importantly, anyone can make it at home. The real deal is to be found at traditional guesthouses and the *Păturată* festivals in the area.

Serves 4–6

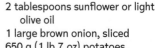

2 tablespoons sunflower or light olive oil
1 large brown onion, sliced
650 g (1 lb 7 oz) potatoes, cut into 1.5 cm (⅔ in) slices, then quartered
1 teaspoon caraway seeds (or fennel seeds)
500 ml (17 fl oz/2 cups) vegetable stock
1 tablespoon chopped fresh dill (optional)

For the Crust

4 medium eggs, beaten
100 g (3½ oz/generous ⅓ cup) thick, Greek-style yoghurt
60 g (2¼ oz) *brânză telemea*, or brined feta-style cheese
5–6 sheets of filo pastry (put the rest back in the packet, store in the refrigerator and use within a week)
70 ml (2½ fl oz/5 tablespoons) sunflower or light olive oil, for brushing
salt and freshly ground black pepper

Heat the oil in a deep, ovenproof 24 cm (9½ in) sauté pan over a medium heat, add the onion and cook for 5 minutes until soft. Add the potatoes and caraway seeds, combine well, then fry for 3 minutes. Add the stock, cover the pan and cook for 15–18 minutes over a medium–low heat until the potatoes soften.

Meanwhile, mix the eggs with the yoghurt and cheese. Add a pinch of salt and a generous pinch of pepper.

Preheat the oven to 170°C fan (325°F/gas 3).

Assemble the crust by building a spiral on a large piece of baking parchment. Take one sheet of filo and brush it with oil. Make creases by folding it from the longer side up, to look like a pleated skirt. Don't be tempted to roll it into a cylinder, you need those creases open to absorb the egg mixture. Now coil it loosely around itself and place it in the middle of the baking parchment. That's the centre of the crust. Repeat with another sheet, and continue the spiral from where you left it, tucking the ends in. Repeat with the rest of the pastry until the spiral reaches the size of the pan. Brush the remaining oil on top.

By now, the potatoes will be ready. Take the pan off the heat and use a fork to crush a quarter of them lightly, then stir a few times to thicken the sauce. You still need a lot of the liquid in the pan to cook the crust. Stir in the dill, if using.

Place the baking parchment with the crust on top of the potatoes and, holding the pie in place with one hand, slide the paper from underneath it with the other. The filo will lose its shape slightly, but you can rearrange it evenly over the potatoes. The spiral looks crinkly anyway.

Use a tablespoon to distribute the egg mixture in between the creases and around the edges of the pastry.

Bake on a lower shelf of the oven for 20 minutes until the crust is golden. It will swell and look gigantic, but it comes back to its senses once it's out of the oven. Remove from the oven and cover with a clean dish towel for 5 minutes.

Use a spatula to release the crust around the edges, and portion the crust carefully with a knife, not slicing all the way down to damage your pan. Serve immediately with a lettuce and rocket (arugula) salad, or pickled red onions.

Mâncare de Mazăre şi Bob cu Frigănele

GARDEN PEA AND BROAD BEAN STEW WITH EGGY BREAD

This is a wonderfully light dish, and when made with seasonal peas and broad (fava) beans, it has a delicious sweet flavour. It is served with eggy bread, *frigănele*, which is a good trick to make a meal more substantial. The aroma that brings everything together is dill, and I know many of you have a love-hate relationship with it, but we love it in Romania. Dill and garden peas are meant to be together. Try it at least once in this combination.

Serves 4

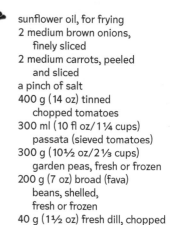

sunflower oil, for frying
2 medium brown onions, finely sliced
2 medium carrots, peeled and sliced
a pinch of salt
400 g (14 oz) tinned chopped tomatoes
300 ml (10 fl oz/1¼ cups) passata (sieved tomatoes)
300 g (10½ oz/2⅓ cups) garden peas, fresh or frozen
200 g (7 oz) broad (fava) beans, shelled, fresh or frozen
40 g (1½ oz) fresh dill, chopped

For the Eggy Bread

4 thick slices of bread
1 large egg, beaten
25 g (1 oz) Romanian *caşcaval* or Cheddar cheese

Heat a thin layer of oil on the base of a deep frying pan (skillet) over a medium heat. Cook the onions and carrots with a pinch of salt until they start to caramelise slightly, then add the tomatoes and passata. Stir well and cook for 5 more minutes, then add the peas and beans together with three-quarters of the dill. Cook until everything is heated evenly.

Meanwhile, soak the bread slices briefly in the beaten egg. Place them on a baking sheet lined with kitchen foil and grate the cheese on top. Put under a hot grill (broiler) for a few minutes until the cheese is melted. If you don't have a grill, fry the soaked bread in oil on both sides, remove onto a warm plate and grate the cheese on top while the slices are still hot.

Serve the eggy bread slices on top of the stew with the rest of the dill sprinkled on top.

Tăiţei cu Varză Murată

WIDE NOODLES WITH SAUERKRAUT

When I was little, I used to insist on mixing the *tăiţei* dough. Mum would then roll the sheets and I would keep checking to see when they were dry enough to be cut into ribbons. It was very exciting. I used to pinch little shreds of raw dough and eat them, and I still like raw pasta even to this day. The dish comes from Transylvania, not that close to the Danube, but it's a glorious vegetarian dish satisfying all cravings for carbs, tanginess and saltiness. It's also good in the summer since fermented ingredients help maintain the right salt levels in the body.

Serves 4

sunflower oil, for frying
1 medium brown onion,
    thinly sliced
500 g (1 lb 2 oz) sauerkraut
400 g (14 oz) flat, wide pasta
    ribbons, such as tagliatelle
    (or make your own *tăiţei*,
    see page 126)
salt and freshly ground
    black pepper

Cover the base of a frying pan (skillet) with a thin layer of oil and heat. Add the onions and cook over a medium heat until soft and translucent, then add the sauerkraut, combine well and turn the heat to low, stirring occasionally.

Cook the pasta in salted boiling water for 12 minutes, or until al dente. If you use homemade pasta, it will only take 3–4 minutes.

Use tongs to transfer the cooked noodles to the frying pan. Mix well with the sauerkraut and onions, adding a few splashes of the cooking liquid if it's not too salty. Otherwise, use water. Remember, sauerkraut can have different levels of saltiness from one brand to another. This dish doesn't actually have a sauce, but you still need a little liquid to bring everything together.

Serve with plenty of pepper.

Tocană Mânăstirească de Legume cu Zabic

MONASTERY VEGETABLE STEW WITH POLENTA CROUTONS

Monastery-style dishes are a combination of whatever seasonal ingredients are available, slow-cooked on the stove or in the oven. Despite the monastic implication, these dishes are not necessarily vegetarian or vegan and can include meat. They are perfect for feeding a crowd and are best enjoyed with bread or polenta to absorb the sauce. I prefer to serve it with *zabic*, a traditional recipe from the south. It involves slicing and frying leftover polenta to be eaten with broths, soups and stews the next day.

Serves 4–6

Start by making a *Mămăligă* Polenta. Transfer it to a shallow 23 cm (9 in) shallow bowl and allow it to cool completely.

Cover the base of a deep, 23 cm (9 in) diameter and 10 cm (4 in) deep cast-iron pan with a thin layer of oil and heat well. Add the onions, carrots and parsnips, and cook over a medium heat for a few minutes, stirring often, until the onions soften. Add the cauliflower and cook for another 3 minutes, then mix in the aubergines and pepper. You can drizzle more oil on top if the pan gets too dry. Turn the heat up for 30 seconds and add the tablespoon of vinegar, allowing it to evaporate for another minute until you can't smell it anymore. Stir in the chopped tomatoes, tomato purée, crumbled stock cube, water, spices and bay leaves. Cover the pot and simmer for 30 minutes over a medium–low heat.

Add the beans and peas, cover the pot again and cook for 10 minutes. Stir in the extra vinegar, taste for seasoning and adjust, then add most of the herbs, reserving a little for serving. It needs to have a good amount of sauce, so add a splash of water if necessary. Cook for another 3 minutes, then turn off the heat.

Make the *zabic* by turning the polenta onto a chopping board. Cut it into 1.5–2 cm (⅔–¾ in) slices, then the same across, so you end up with different-sized cubes. Heat the butter and oil in a large frying pan (skillet) over a high heat. Add the cubes and fry for 10 minutes, tossing and turning them gently, until they form a golden crust.

Serve with the stew, sprinkling the rest of the herbs on top.

For the Zabic Polenta Croutons

1 batch of *Mămăligă* Polenta (see page 15)
25 g (1 oz) salted butter
1 tablespoon sunflower oil

For the Stew

sunflower oil, for frying
2 medium brown onions, sliced
2 medium carrots, sliced into discs
2 medium parsnips, quartered
1 medium cauliflower, cut into florets
1 medium aubergine (eggplant), cut into 2 cm (¾ in) chunks
1 medium yellow (bell) pepper, sliced
1 tablespoon white wine vinegar, plus 2 teaspoons to add at the end
400 g (14 oz) tinned chopped tomatoes
scant 2 tablespoons tomato purée (paste)
1 vegetable stock cube
300 ml (10 fl oz/ 1¼ cups) water
1 teaspoon sweet paprika
½ teaspoon chilli powder
3 bay leaves
180 g (6½ oz) fine green beans
100 g (3½ oz/⅔ cup) garden peas, fresh or frozen
1 tablespoon chopped dill
1 tablespoon chopped parsley
salt and freshly ground black pepper

Ardei Umpluți cu Linte si Bulgur

LENTIL AND BURGHUL WHEAT STUFFED PEPPERS

In Romania, we have an obsession with stuffing vegetables. Whatever grows in the garden, we don't hesitate to hollow out and stuff with rice, meat, fruit, pulses or beans. Stuffed peppers tend to be more a part of a home cook's repertoire rather than that of a chef in a restaurant. This recipe brings together two historic ingredients that are seeing a comeback in our cuisine: burghul wheat and lentils.

Serves 4

Heat a thin layer of oil on the base of a deep pan. Turn the heat to low and cook the onions with a pinch of salt until soft. Add the burghul wheat, tarragon and water, and simmer for 6–8 minutes until the water is absorbed and the burghul is cooked. Take the pan off the heat, add the butter, lentils and carrots, combine well and set aside to cool. Add another generous pinch of salt, taste and adjust the seasoning again.

Heat a large non-stick frying pan (skillet) that also has a lid. Add the peppers whole and cook, turning often on all sides, until they start to soften and become more flexible. Don't cook them all the way through. Set aside to cool.

For the sauce, cover the base of the pan with another thin layer of oil and heat well. Add the onions and a pinch of salt, and cook over a medium heat until they are translucent. Add the tomatoes and paprika, bringing everything to the boil. Taste and adjust the level of salt.

By now, the peppers should have cooled, so cut off the ends with the stalk, gently remove the seeds inside, then stuff each pepper with the filling. I use my fingers to push in as much filling as I can. Place them in the sauce, cover the pan and cook over a medium–low heat for 25–30 minutes until the peppers are soft.

Serve sprinkled with fresh tarragon and a dollop of sour cream, yoghurt or crème fraîche.

For the Filling

sunflower oil, for frying
2 medium brown onions, sliced
50 g (2 oz/¼ cup)
    burghul wheat
2 teaspoons dried tarragon
125 ml (4 fl oz/½ cup) water
50 g (2 oz) salted butter
260 g (9½ oz) tinned
    cooked lentils
2 medium carrots, grated
4 large Romano peppers
salt, to taste

For the Sauce

sunflower oil, for frying
2 medium brown onions, sliced
a pinch of salt, or to taste
2 x 400 g (14 oz) tins of
    chopped tomatoes
½ teaspoon hot paprika

To Serve

fresh tarragon, chopped
sour cream, thick yoghurt
    or crème fraîche

A LAND OF VEGETABLES

Sarmale cu Păsat

MILLET AND MUSHROOM STUFFED VINE LEAVES

Sarmale, stuffed leaves, are a whole category of dishes in Romanian cuisine. They are a world of their own, generous and inventive, using not just sauerkraut or vine leaves but linden, lovage, dock, horseradish and even raspberry leaves. The fillings vary from meat to vegan, not just pork and beef, but duck and fish and even whelks; not just rice but dried fruit, nuts and cheese. They are usually simmered in tomato sauce or stock, and served as a main course with sour cream and polenta or mashed potatoes. In Gorj, a county in southern Romania, they are accompanied by cold aspic dishes called *răcituri*. Still in the south, including in my father's village, people stuff cabbage leaves with *păsat*, cornmeal so coarsely ground that it looks similar to rice grains. I love it for its many flavour contrasts and textures. For practical reasons, my recipe takes the easy and more accessible route of using vine leaves and millet.

Serves 4–6 (makes 22–28 rolls of various sizes)

350 g (12 oz) vine leaves
1 litre (34 fl oz/4½ cups)
    vegetable stock
150 g (5 oz/scant ⅔ cup)
    sour cream
1 teaspoon chopped dill,
    to garnish (optional)

For the Filling

225 g (8 oz/scant
    1½ cups) millet
600 ml (20 fl oz/2½ cups) water
25 g (1 oz) salted butter
sunflower oil, for frying
2 medium brown onions, sliced
250 g (9 oz) fresh
    mushrooms, diced
1 teaspoon finely chopped fresh
    or dried sage
salt and freshly ground
    black pepper

Make the filling by simmering the millet in water for 20 minutes, until soft but not mushy. Stir in the butter and set aside. Cover the base of a frying pan with a thin layer of oil and cook the onions with a pinch of salt until softened. Add the mushrooms and sage and cook for 10 more minutes, then mix it with the millet and allow to cool. Prepare the vine leaves by separating them one by one. Remove the tough stalks, place the leaf pointing away from you and fill it with 1 or 2 teaspoons of millet, bringing the sides towards the middle as you roll. Shred the smaller leaves and place them on the base of the pan, then arrange the rolls on top. Add the stock, shake the pan so it distributes evenly, then simmer for 45 minutes. Serve hot with sour cream, dill, bread or mashed potatoes.

Note

Sarmale are a national dish throughout the Balkans and in Romania. The method of wrapping meat in leaves to protect it from the direct heat of fire or hot water was already known, but the Ottoman Empire made the name popular. Historian Özge Samanci finds the first mentions of *sarma* in 16th-century Turkish cookery books, where the recipes were perfected from Persian cuisine using meat. Later vegetarian versions using rice were inspired by the Greek and Armenian communities in Istanbul and their Lent dishes.

Legume cu Bulgur la Cuptor

BURGHUL WHEAT WITH ROASTED VEGETABLES

In Dobrogea, the transition from fishing to farming villages is sudden. Neighbouring villages can be completely different in their way of living and eating. I stayed in Vişina, where, despite being next door to the fishing village of Jurilovca, people eat grains, vegetables and meat. Fish dishes are rare and not traditional. The place is only a little more inland from the Razim lagoon, and most people are from the Bulgarian ethnic groups. One afternoon, my host, Bianca Folescu, who runs a Museum of Rural Life and a guesthouse, pulled out an old book listing the locals' diet at the beginning of the 20th century. We found that in these inland areas, burghul wheat was historically favoured over rice. Here is a recipe inspired by our conversation in the shade of a cooling reed roof on a hot September's day. It brings together the elements of cooking in old Vişina village.

Serves 4

olive oil, for cooking
1 large leek, sliced
300 g (10½ oz/1¾ cups) coarse burghul wheat
2 medium garlic cloves, sliced
600 ml (20 fl oz/2½ cups) vegetable stock
1 medium aubergine (eggplant), cut into 1.5 cm (⅔ in) slices
1 red (bell) pepper, sliced
1 yellow (bell) pepper, sliced
1 tablespoon chopped fresh parsley
salt and freshly ground black pepper

Preheat the oven to 200°C fan (400°F/gas 6).

Heat a thin layer of oil in a 24 cm (9½ in) ovenproof pan over a medium heat and fry the leek with a pinch of salt for 3 minutes, stirring often. Add the burghul wheat and garlic, combine well and cook for another 2 minutes. Pour in the stock, add 1 teaspoon salt, and bring to the boil. Set aside.

In a bowl, toss the aubergines and peppers with a generous amount of olive oil and a pinch of salt and pepper. Distribute evenly on top of the burghul (which will look a bit watery at this stage – that's fine). Bake on a middle shelf of the oven for 20 minutes. Remove from the oven and drizzle more olive oil on top.

Serve immediately, seasoned with black pepper and sprinkled with chopped parsley. It goes well with a tomato and rocket (arugula) salad or steamed greens.

Note

You can also use a frying pan (skillet) to sauté the leeks, then transfer them with the burghul and stock to a 24 cm (9½ in) pie dish.

A LAND OF VEGETABLES

A LAND

OF
FISHERMEN

Fishing in the Danube Delta

It is in this delta that the mighty Danube river ends its journey through Europe, from the Black Forest of Germany to the Black Sea in Romania. It is a landscape dominated by marshes, canals and reed islands, and – of course – by fish. The Black Sea abounds in herring, mackerel and anchovies, but it's the freshwater fish of the Danube that matter most.

Here, carp is the most popular fish, prized for its white, rich flesh, then trout, perch, shad, zander, pike, eel and catfish. Mullet and turbot like fresh and saltwater, so they live in river deltas and brackish estuaries. This is also the case of sturgeon, the most iconic fish of all, now protected by an indefinite fishing ban. The species is almost extinct because of the intense harvesting of its roe, having produced the world's most expensive caviar. Sturgeon is currently farmed, which allows people to keep their traditions by preparing historic recipes such as *storceag*. This fish soup is made only with sturgeon and is associated with the Lipoveni communities in the Delta.

In Romania, fish is traditionally prepared whole with the head on if the size is reasonable, or cut into steaks if it's too large. It is never deboned before cooking. We love fish on the bone, and many people in Romania know how to remove them when they eat. I learned when I was little, and to this day I've had no accidents. The most popular cooking method is frying, and we like to roll the fish in cornmeal, which gives it a nice, golden crust. The cornmeal absorbs some of the oil, and the skin turns into the most delicious crackling. The tail fin gets really crispy, which is a delicacy for many people, including myself. It can also be prepared on a bed of salt on a flat iron or, of course, it can be poached in soups.

In the following recipes, I use fish widely accessible to a Western market to make them practical.

A Way of Life

In the past, being a fisherman in the Delta was a solitary occupation. Out on the river all season, following the fish shoals and living on the narrow strips of land between the waters, they rarely emerged into their communities or showed up at their own homes. Their only contact with the world was at a *cherhana*, a fish sorting hub where they unloaded their catch.

Camping on the river banks when night fell offered very little in terms of cooking. Usually, fishermen would pack up a cauldron in their boat for boiling and a flat iron for grilling (broiling). They had maize to make polenta, since it was quicker than making bread, and some garlic to make the sauce required to cut through the fattiness of the fish. Bread was only bought on rare occasions or baked in communal clay ovens built along the river banks.

Their staple dish was a sour soup, called *ciorbă* or *borş*, made with any fish they didn't sell at the collection points. So, they also carried with them a sour ingredient, verjus from unripe grapes, vinegar or small sachets of citric acid, which helped to firm up the fish flesh. If they had any vegetables, such as potatoes, onions and tomatoes, it was a good day. If not, they relied on foraged plants, especially wild lovage, which today is an indisputable ingredient in the preparation of *ciorbă* (see page 115). The fish was used whole or cut into chunks, while the intestines and the fish eggs were fried like fritters. Snacks were prepared from cooked water chestnuts and the roots of water lilies. This way of life generated the most iconic dishes of the Delta that everyone enjoys today.

Jumări de Pește

FRIED SALMON MORSELS WITH PAPRIKA ONION SALAD AND POTATO WEDGES

Jumări means 'fried morsels', usually cuts of meat with a good fat content such as pork scratchings and belly. They can also be made with carp or catfish, especially using the fatty belly, if the fish is large. I tested the recipe with salmon for practical reasons and the result was very good. It is a dish that can be served on its own as a starter or with drinks, or as a main course with potatoes and salad.

Serves 4

Place the sliced onions for the salad in a bowl, add the salt and vinegar, and mix well. Before serving, adjust the seasoning and vinegar if necessary, then sprinkle with paprika. On its own, the salad is very sharp, but when served with the rest of the dish, it works a treat.

Preheat the oven to 200°C fan (400°F/gas 6).

Pour the oil into a large roasting pan that will accommodate the potatoes in one layer. Heat in the oven for a couple of minutes, then add the potatoes. Season generously and toss the potatoes until they are very well coated in oil. Roast for 30 minutes on the middle shelf.

Remove the potatoes from the oven, sprinkle the semolina and thyme on top, drizzle with a little more oil and combine everything together well. Adjust the seasoning if necessary. Return to the oven and roast for 10 more minutes, or until the potatoes are golden with crisp edges.

Now turn your attention to the salmon – it won't take more than 10 minutes to prepare it. Cut the fish into 3–4 cm (1–1½ in) cubes or chunks. You can remove the skin if you like, but it turns delicious in the pan. Season the pieces generously and toss them well in the flour. Heat a thin layer of oil in the base of a frying pan (skillet) and throw in the salmon pieces. Fry for about 5 minutes over a medium–high heat, turning on all sides. Do this in batches if you can't put them all in the pan in one layer. Remove to a sieve (fine mesh strainer) placed on top of a bowl.

Serve the fried salmon immediately with the potatoes and onion salad on the side, with lemon wedges for squeezing.

For the Paprika Onion Salad

2 medium brown onions, thinly sliced
½ teaspoon salt
4 teaspoons white wine vinegar
½ teaspoon paprika

For the Potato Wedges

2½ tablespoons sunflower oil, plus extra as needed
800 g (1 lb 12 oz) medium potatoes, cut into wedges
1 tablespoon semolina
20 g (¾ oz) thyme, leaves picked and finely chopped
salt and freshly ground black pepper

For the Fish

500 g (1 lb 2 oz) boneless side of salmon or fillets
1 tablespoon plain (all-purpose) flour
sunflower oil, for frying
salt and freshly ground black pepper
lemon wedges, to serve

Rapane Pané

BREADED WHELKS WITH YOGHURT SALAD

This is a dish from the Black Sea, southern Dobrogea, and provides a rare occasion for many people on holiday by the sea to eat whelks. If you prefer to stay in a guesthouse instead of a luxury hotel, you can even pick the whelks yourself and prepare them in the summer kitchen on the grill (broiler) or in the pan. The yoghurt salad is my addition from across the border in Bulgaria, where it is known as a dry version of *tarator*. Its white colour attracted the name Snow White, *Snezhanka*, and is a refreshing accompaniment to this light lunch on a hot day.

Serves 4

Start by making the salad. Put the yoghurt in a sieve (fine-mesh strainer) set over a bowl and allow it to drain, removing as much whey as possible. It takes around 30 minutes or you can leave it overnight. Mix the strained yoghurt with the cucumbers, grate the garlic on top and add the rest of the ingredients. Combine well and taste, adjusting the seasoning and garlic flavour if you need.

Heat a thick layer of oil in the base of a frying pan (skillet) over a high heat. I use a small pan and work in batches. While the oil is heating, add a pinch of salt to the whelks, toss them in flour thoroughly, then place them in a sieve to shake off the excess flour. Place the egg and breadcrumbs in two separate bowls. Dip the whelks in the beaten egg and use a slotted spoon or your hands to transfer them to the dish with the breadcrumbs, allowing the wash to run off. Coat them in the breadcrumbs, then put them into the hot oil, leaving any extra breadcrumbs in the dish. Turn the heat to medium and fry, tossing them around, for about 4–5 minutes until golden and crisp. Transfer to a sieve set over a bowl to drain excess oil.

Serve immediately, with flatbread, generous dollops of the yoghurt salad and, if you wish, lemony lettuce leaves.

For the Yoghurt Salad

250 g (9 oz/ 1 cup) thick
    plain yoghurt
100 g (3½ oz) cucumber,
    peeled and finely diced
1 large garlic clove
60 g (2¼ oz/½ cup)
    chopped walnuts
1 teaspoon chopped fresh dill
    or tarragon, lovage, parsley
a drizzle of oil
1 teaspoon white wine vinegar

For the Whelks

sunflower oil, for frying
500 g (1 lb 2 oz) pre-cooked
    whelks
a pinch of salt
80 g (3 oz/⅔ cup) plain
    (all-purpose) flour
2 medium eggs, beaten
80 g (3 oz/¾ cup) golden
    breadcrumbs

To Serve

flatbreads
lemon-dressed lettuce leaves
    (optional)

Pește cu Mujdei

PAN-FRIED SEA BREAM WITH GARLIC SAUCE AND POLENTA

In Romania, the most common way to prepare fish at home is to fry it. We serve it with a good garlic sauce to awaken the flavours and with a soft polenta to bring everything together. In restaurants, fish can also be grilled (broiled) and served with fries and a tomato salad.

Serves 2–4

For the Garlic Sauce

20 g (¾ oz) garlic cloves, peeled
1 teaspoon fine salt, or to taste
2 tablespoons oil (sunflower, olive or a mixture of both)
2 teaspoons white wine vinegar
1 tablespoon freshly chopped parsley, tarragon, lovage, fennel, dill or a mixture of all, plus extra to garnish
150 ml (5 fl oz/scant ⅔ cup) water

For the Fish

2 small whole sea bream
50 g (2 oz/scant ½ cup) plain (all-purpose) flour
50 g (2 oz/⅓ cup) medium-ground cornmeal
1 teaspoon salt
sunflower oil, for frying

To Serve

1 batch of *Mămăligă* Polenta (see page 15)

For the sauce, crush the garlic with the salt in a pestle and mortar. Add the oil, 1 tablespoon at a time, mixing well with the pestle to a creamy consistency. Add the vinegar and stir everything well. Add the parsley (or other herbs), crushing lightly with the pestle, then stir in the water. Taste for seasoning, it needs to be quite salty. Set aside.

Wash the fish with cold water inside and out, and pat dry. Mix the flour and cornmeal and transfer to a large plate. Sprinkle the salt on both sides of the fish and inside, then roll and coat the fish in the flour mixture.

Heat a good layer of oil in a frying pan (skillet) that is large enough to accommodate the fish over a medium–high heat. Add the fish, shaking the pan to avoid it sticking to the base. Cook for 4 minutes, then turn very carefully to the other side and cook for a further 4 minutes until the crust is golden.

Meanwhile, make the *Mămăligă* Polenta following the instructions on page 15. Keep the pan covered until you are ready to serve.

Serve the fish immediately with spoonfuls of garlic sauce on top next to the polenta (or steamed potatoes or fries) and garnished with extra herbs.

Papricaș de Pește

FISH PAPRIKASH WITH EGG DUMPLINGS

When people hear about *papricaș*, they immediately think of the famous Hungarian chicken dish with tomatoes and paprika. Yet you will find carp or catfish paprikash in traditional restaurants in Budapest, the majestic Danubian capital city of Hungary. It is served with *nokeldi*, a German name popular in Central and Eastern Europe, that describes any type of dumpling.

Serves 4

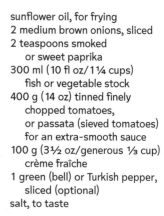

sunflower oil, for frying
2 medium brown onions, sliced
2 teaspoons smoked
    or sweet paprika
300 ml (10 fl oz/1¼ cups)
    fish or vegetable stock
400 g (14 oz) tinned finely
    chopped tomatoes,
    or passata (sieved tomatoes)
    for an extra-smooth sauce
100 g (3½ oz/generous ⅓ cup)
    crème fraîche
1 green (bell) or Turkish pepper,
    sliced (optional)
salt, to taste

For the Dumplings

250 g (9 oz/2 cups) plain
    (all-purpose) flour
2 large eggs
100 ml (3½ fl oz/scant ½ cup)
    cold water
1 teaspoon salt, plus extra
    for cooking

For the Fish

sunflower oil, for frying
4 medium cod loins or a similar
    white fish

Heat a thin layer of oil on the base of a sauté pan or casserole dish with a lid over a medium heat.

Add the onions with a pinch of salt and cook for 8–10 minutes until soft and translucent. Mix in the paprika quickly to avoid burning and pour over the stock together with the chopped tomatoes. Bring to the boil, then reduce the heat to low. Taste and adjust the seasoning.

Make the dumplings by mixing all the ingredients. Bring a large pan of well-salted water to the boil. Dip a teaspoon into the water and start scooping up small amounts of the dumpling mix. Half a teaspoon is usually a good size but don't worry if you make them larger. Put as many as possible in the pan of water to form a single layer on the base of the pan. Boil until they pop up to the surface, around 3–4 minutes. Use a slotted spoon to transfer the dumplings to the paprika sauce, and repeat with the rest of the mixture. Coat them well in the sauce every time you add a new batch. Stir in the crème fraîche.

Heat a thin layer of oil in a pan large enough to accommodate the fish. Pat the cod dry and fry for a couple of minutes on each side. Flake and tuck it among the dumplings and serve with slices of green pepper on top.

Cetățile Dobrogei, The Fortified Towns of Ancient Dobrogea

Dobrogea was one of the most fortified frontiers of the Roman Empire. Its location, offering access to the Danube river and the Black Sea made it a strategic region for settlers and merchants even before the Roman times. If you decide to travel here, it is the equivalent of Egypt's Valley of the Kings, with over 300 sites of historical importance, their relics and walls dating from as far back as the Bronze Age.

By the 7th century BC, Ionian Greeks from Asia Minor had established colonies along the Danube and Black Sea coastline, close to local Getae tribes. They made a living by fishing and harvesting salt, selling salted fish, wheat, wine, honey and wax in return for luxury goods from their homelands.

An important activity was winemaking, and the Greeks introduced an unusual grape that is now considered indigenous to Romania, called Tămâioasă, still producing an exotic-tasting wine today. When the Roman Empire conquered the colonies, they continued to grow grapes and also expanded the infrastructure and agriculture through their system of villages and *villae rusticae* farmhouses. Today, the lands have been included in the Roman Emperors and Danube Wine Route, established by the Council of Europe in 2015 to connect archaeological sites to modern vineyards where the Romans produced wine.

In later centuries, more people came to this diverse and flourishing part of the Danube to rule, such as the Ottomans, or to trade or find refuge, such as the Greeks, Armenians, Genoese and Jews but also Tatars, Bulgarians, Macedonians, Russians and even Italians.

When I travelled through this region, I stayed in a village called Vișina, near Razim Lake, a saltwater lagoon created by the Black Sea. My host, Bianca Folescu, made me a dinner to enjoy the local flavours: fried fish with cornmeal crust, served with polenta and garlic sauce (see recipe on page 175), locally grown vegetables and a filo cheese pie called *Dobrogeană* (see the recipe on page 60). So, I felt I had to work it all out by exploring the area the next day.

Argamum Fortress

I reached Argamum via an off-road track, starting in Jurilovca. It is the oldest fortress to be mentioned in written ancient sources, and it sits right on the edge of Dolojman Head, a promontory of steep rocks offering a fantastic view of the saltwater lagoons on the Black Sea. Greek colonists built it in the 7th century BC over an old Bronze Age settlement and called it Orgame. This was where the Argonauts were believed to have stopped on their way home after finding the Golden Fleece, so the Romans called it Argamum. Its excavation started in 1916 and led to the discovery of the oldest necropolis on the Black Sea coastline. With three Christian basilicas and traces of commerce with Byzantium, many people think it is the cradle of Christianity in Romania. Looking at it like that, I think the whole of Dobrogea is the cradle of our faith.

Enisala Fortress

Called *Yeni-Sale* in Turkish, it was built in medieval times by Genoese merchants, who wanted to control and defend the maritime traffic on the Black Sea, over which they had a monopoly. Other sources say it was a military fortress for the Tatars of the Golden Horde since it sat right on top of a steep, stony hill affording views for miles around. Today, it is one of the most visited fortresses in the region, and I was impressed by the panoramic view of the natural reserve at Enisala with its surreal landscape.

All the ancient sites of Dobrogea are magical, just reading through their names you are transported deep back in time: Histria, Tomis, Callatis, Sacidava, Tropeum Traiani, Axiopolis, Dinogetia, Carsium, Beroe and many others.

Musaca de Peşte

FISH MOUSSAKA

When you travel to Dobrogea and ask people what they are going to make for dinner that evening, the answer is often a *musaca*. Inland, this dish is made with aubergines (eggplants), potatoes and meat, while in the Danube Delta you can find this version with fish. I had mine many years ago when holidaying in Sfântu Gheorghe village, where the river meets the sea and you can only get there by ferry. In those days, it was a place of wilderness, most of us were camping on the beach or staying with locals. In the meantime, an important open-air film festival has been taking place here every year, and many hotels have sprung up with their modern offerings and menus. However, I was happy to learn that many tourists still prefer to dine in local kitchens to experience traditional cooking methods.

Serves 4–6

500 g (1 lb 2 oz) potatoes
500 g (1 lb 2 oz) aubergines (eggplants), (around 2 medium)
sunflower oil, for frying and brushing
2 medium onions, sliced
3 large garlic cloves, sliced
380 g (13 oz) white fish fillets, cod or haddock, cut into chunks (or fish pie mix)
1 tablespoon plain (all-purpose) flour
300 g (10½ oz) tinned chopped tomatoes
25g (1 oz) capers, plus 1 teaspoon of their brine
1 teaspoon chopped fresh mint
salt and freshly ground black pepper

For the Topping

200 g (7 oz/generous ¾ cup) sour cream
1 medium egg
1½ tablespoons plain (all-purpose) flour
extra capers (optional)

Fill a large pan with water, add 2 generous pinches of salt and bring to the boil. Slice the potatoes very thinly, using a mandoline or the slicing disc of your food processor. Put them in the boiling water, turn the heat to medium and cook for 8–10 minutes. Remove with a slotted spoon to a large plate lined with paper towel. Use the same water to blanch the aubergines, which should be cut into 5 mm–1 cm (¼–½ in) slices. Cook for a few minutes until they start to soften in the middle, then remove to another plate lined with paper towel. Sprinkle with a pinch of salt.

Preheat the oven to 180°C fan (350°F/gas 4).

Heat a thin layer of oil in the base of a saucepan. Add the onions with a pinch of salt and cook over a medium heat until they start to caramelise slightly. Add the garlic and cook for a few more minutes until the garlic smells sweet and less pungent. Toss the fish chunks in the flour and add them to the onion mix. (Make sure you don't add the surplus flour left in the bowl.) Cook for 2 minutes, shaking the pan and moving the fish around gently. Add the chopped tomatoes, capers, brine and mint, adjust for salt and pepper, simmer for 5 more minutes, then turn the heat off.

Assemble the pie in a 26 x 18 cm (11 x 7 in) ovenproof dish (glass, ceramic or tin). Brush the base with a small amount of oil, then arrange half of the potatoes on the base, overlapping them slightly. Do the same with the aubergines. Spread the fish sauce over evenly, then arrange the rest of the potatoes and aubergines on top.

For the topping, mix together the sour cream, egg and flour, and pour it over the moussaka. Dot some extra capers on top if you wish.

Bake for 35 minutes on a lower shelf. Remove and allow it to calm down from the heat of the oven for a few minutes, then serve.

Chiftelușe de Pește

DILL FISHCAKES

This recipe is somewhere between fish cakes and fish croquettes, and allows the flavour of the fish to stay as clear as possible without being mixed with potatoes, rice and other ingredients. We usually serve fish with a salad and I've suggested three here for you to choose from.

Makes 10 fishcakes

sunflower oil, for frying
1 medium brown onion, sliced
a pinch of salt
2 medium garlic cloves, sliced
500 g (1 lb 2 oz) white fish
    or fish pie mix
2 medium eggs
1 tbsp chopped dill (or fennel
    herb), plus extra to garnish
zest of 1 medium lemon
100 g (3½ oz/1 cup)
    golden breadcrumbs

To Serve

Potato and Egg Salad with
    Olives (see page 88)
Vlach Fried Pepper Salad
    (see page 103)
Crème Fraîche, Cucumber and
    Lettuce Salad (see page 111)

Heat a thin layer of oil in a frying pan (skillet) over a medium heat. Add the onion with a pinch of salt and cook until beginning to caramelise. Add the garlic and cook for a couple more minutes, then set aside.

In a food processor, blitz the fish with one of the eggs, herbs, lemon zest, cooked onion and garlic. (If you use frozen fish, especially the pie mix, you will need to defrost it first, then place it in a sieve(fine mesh strainer) and press on it gently to squeeze all the water out.) If the mixture is too dry, add the second egg and blitz again. The mixture should be soft when raw; it will firm up during cooking.

Spread the breadcrumbs on a plate. Heat a generous layer of oil on the base of a large frying pan over a medium heat. Oil your hands and shape 10 patties out of the fish mixture, about 8–10 cm (3–4 in) in diameter, then coat in breadcrumbs. Shape and slide them into the hot oil as you go along. Cook the fishcakes for 4 minutes on each side until firm to the touch and with a golden crust. Adjust the heat up or down, as needed, to avoid burning the cakes on the outside.

Garnish with extra dill and serve with any of the salads mentioned opposite.

Pilaf Marea Neagră

BLACK SEA ORZO AND TOASTED VERMICELLI PILAF WITH HADDOCK

This is a wonderful dish inspired by the Turkish and Tatar cuisines in Dobrogea, where they combine orzo with vermicelli pasta in dishes called *botqa*. Although most of them are made to accompany meat, I use the recipe with fish.

Serves 4

15 g (½ oz) unsalted butter
170 g (6 oz) vermicelli pasta
sunflower oil, for frying
500 g (1 lb 2 oz) leeks, sliced, green tops included
a pinch of salt
150 g (5 oz/¾ cup) orzo
600 ml (20 fl oz/2½ cups) well-flavoured, clear fish stock
400 g (14 oz) unsmoked or smoked haddock misshapes, skinned and boned
1 tablespoon chopped parsley or fennel herb

Melt the butter in a frying pan (skillet) and cook the vermicelli pasta for 10 minutes until golden, tossing often. Set aside.

Heat a thin layer of oil on the base of a 24 cm (9½ in) sauté pan over a medium heat. Cook the leeks with a generous pinch of salt for 8 minutes until they start to soften and their green colour intensifies. Mix in the orzo and cook for a couple more minutes, then add 150 g (5 oz) of the vermicelli pasta (reserving 20 g /¾ oz for serving) and 500 ml (17 fl oz/2 cups) of the stock, reserving 100 ml (3½ fl oz/scant ½ cup) for when you add the fish. Turn the heat to low, cover the pan and simmer for 10–12 minutes until the orzo and pasta are soft. Stir gently a few times to make sure that the rice doesn't catch on the bottom of the pan.

Place the fish on top and tuck it well into the pilaf, then add the rest of the stock. Shake the pan gently, cover and cook for another 5 minutes. The fish is cooked when it looks opaque and you can flake it easily with a fork. Sprinkle with the chopped herbs and reserved vermicelli and serve immediately with a fresh lettuce salad or quick vinegar pickles.

Saramură de Pește

SALT-BAKED RAINBOW TROUT WITH TOMATO DRESSING AND POLENTA

This is a popular way to prepare fish, and you will find it in many restaurants and homes throughout the country regardless of their proximity to water. A *saramură* is a brine, the name comes from *sal* meaning 'salt'. Originally a fisherman's dish, it was made with whatever fish they had caught and was not good to sell. In its simplest form, the dish is grilled fish on a hot plate or a bed of salt, served in a brine dressing with polenta. A fisherman out on the river for weeks following the fish banks would have had a kettle for boiling and maybe a hot plate for grilling (broiling), nothing else (see page 169). A more sophisticated version is to add tomatoes, peppers, garlic and herbs.

Serves 2–4

Make the sauce by combining all the ingredients in a bowl. Taste and adjust the vinegar, as it needs to be quite tangy. The sauce doesn't require cooking.

Preheat the oven to 200°C fan (400°F/gas 6). Cover the base of a large baking sheet with a generous layer of coarse salt. When the oven is at temperature, place the baking sheet on a lower shelf for 5 minutes.

Wash the trout inside and out, and sprinkle with a pinch of salt inside before stuffing it with lemon slices. It is not necessary to drizzle with oil. Place the fish on the bed of salt and bake for 5 minutes. Remove from the oven, carefully turn the fish onto the other side and bake for another 5 minutes. Repeat one more time. The last time you turn it, you will see that the skin has some scorched patches, which is fine.

Meanwhile, make the *Mămăligă* Polenta and keep it covered on a very low heat until ready to serve.

When the fish is ready, boil a kettle of water.

Choose a large platter, at least 5 cm (2 in) deep, to serve the fish in. As soon as the trout is out of the oven, transfer it to this dish. Pour hot water around the fish just to cover the base of the dish, then pour the tomato sauce over the fish. Shake the dish a little to allow some of the sauce to mix with the water. Serve half a fish per person, with generous amounts of sauce and polenta.

For the Sauce

300 g (10½ oz) grated fresh tomatoes or tinned finely chopped tomatoes
½ teaspoon fine salt
2 medium garlic cloves, grated
1 small green chilli pepper, finely sliced, or ¼ teaspoon chilli powder
1 tablespoon white wine vinegar, or to taste
1 tablespoon finely chopped parsley

For the Fish

75 g (2½ oz/generous ½ cup) coarse sea salt, or more
2 medium rainbow trout, whole
a pinch of salt
1 medium lemon, sliced

To serve

1 batch of *Mămăliga* Polenta (see page 15)

Malasolca

POACHED SALTED FISH WITH POTATOES AND SARMUZAC GARLIC SAUCE

This dish comes from the Lipoveni communities in Northern Dobrogea, and it means 'a little salt'. When fish is plentiful, it is traditional to preserve it by salting or smoking it to be used in dishes throughout the rest of the year. It is served with boiled whole potatoes and two sauces: garlic *sarmuzac* sauce and horseradish sauce. *Sarmuzac* is a garlic mousse based on the garlic's properties to emulsify beautifully when mixed with oil. In Romania, we use raw garlic, but I adjusted the recipe for more sensitive palates. I also offer two types of fish, that together will bring the flavours closer to the original. The dish is a stunning example of simplicity and fishermen's culinary wisdom.

Serves 4

Desalinate the salted cod according to the instructions on the packet. It usually takes 24 hours of soaking in cold water.

Make the *sarmuzac* sauce by heating the oil in a small pan. Add the garlic cloves and tilt the pan so that they are submerged in the oil for a few seconds. Turn the heat off, leave for 10 minutes, then remove the cloves to a pestle and mortar. Crush them to a paste with a pinch of salt. Add the oil, little by little, using the pestle to stir and emulsify the mixture. Stir in the lemon juice. It should have the consistency of extra-thick double (heavy) cream. Set aside.

Put the potatoes in a large pan, cover with water and bring to the boil. Add a few pinches of salt and cook until soft.

Meanwhile, in a separate pan, cover the cod (which was previously desalinated) with water, add the bay leaves and onions, and simmer for 15 minutes until soft and cooked through but not mushy. Do the same with the kippers in just plain water. Transfer the cod to paper towel, pat dry and remove any bones, then cut into pieces. You can serve the kippers whole, or remove the head, skin and some of the bones.

Serve with the boiled potatoes and onions, garlic *sarmuzac* and creamed horseradish. I sometimes drizzle some olive oil over the fish and scatter over some parsley or lovage, which is not traditional but so good.

500 g (1 lb 2 oz) salted cod
800 g (1 lb 12 oz) new potatoes, whole, skin on and washed
3–4 bay leaves
2 medium brown onions, peeled and cut into quarters
2 smoked kippers
1 tablespoon chopped parsley or lovage
salt

For the Sarmuzac Sauce

60 ml (2 fl oz/¼ cup) sunflower or olive oil
60 g (2¼ oz) garlic cloves, peeled
a pinch of salt
juice of 1 medium lemon

To Serve

creamed horseradish

Note

You can choose to make this recipe with only one type of fish, and if you like it, make it again following the recipe.

A LAND

OF
SHEPHERDS

Tatars in Dobrogea

Switch on the TV when you are in Romania and you'll soon find yourself watching a programme about the rich ethnic diversity of our culture. Journalists report live from events across the country, showing local folk dancers and music bands performing on stage and busy crowds browsing the stalls sampling local ethnic dishes. But this wasn't the case 30-plus years ago. Growing up in Romania under the Communist regime, a veil had been drawn over our ethnic heritage, and I knew nothing about it. For many years, during our summer holidays at the Black Sea, on the rare occasion when clouds ruined our beach day, my family would take my sister and I on short trips to explore the region. It was in Constanța that I first visited a mosque, and came to realise why it was there, but I didn't hear the call to prayer or people speaking Tatar language like we hear today.

The Tatar, together with the Turkish ethnic groups, represent the Muslim faith in Romania and are predominant in Dobrogea. Although both groups are similar in many aspects, especially religion, their historical context is different. While the Ottoman Turks were here to rule, the Tatar groups came here to find refuge. I'm referring to the Crimean Tatars, known in Dobrogea as Kirim, and to the Nogay clans. They were driven to these lands by the break up of the Golden Horde and later by the Crimean War and Russian ethnic cleansing, which sadly is practised to this day. Originally, the Tatars were Turkic-speaking nomadic tribes called Cumans or Qipchaq, hence the alternative name of the Crimean Khanate was the Qipchaq Khanate.

Historian Alexandru Chiselev, in his book about the ethnic traditions of Dobrogea, finds that Tatars today see their migration here as an enormous chance to live according to their religion and to keep their identity. It is said that when they left Crimea, they took the embers of the home ancestral fire with them and kept it burning all the way to Dobrogea. The Tatars believed that the perpetual flames of the hearth were a symbol of continuity and life, so they carried the embers in metal pots or whatever they had, and brought it to their new homeland.

At the Tatar Table

Reflecting the tumultuous history of Dobrogean Tatars, the cuisine is a blend of nomadic customs and Ottoman and Romanian influences. Here, people were cattle herders and sheep farmers, so dishes were dominated by meat, beef or mutton, and fermented dairy like yoghurt. Where the land permitted, they grew wheat to extract the flour needed for bread, noodles and pastries.

The most iconic Tatar dish in Dobrogea is Şuberec, a fried thin pastry stuffed with minced (ground) lamb (see page 67). Many meat-stuffed pastries and breads, including the leavened buns Geantîk (see page 70) are served with fresh fruit in the summer and poached dried fruit in the winter.

Pasta dumplings filled with meat are popular and considered a form of culinary art. Women take pride in making them as small as possible. When served in a soup called Tatar aşî, the dumplings are known as qaşiq borek because they are eaten with a spoon. When served as a main dish, they are called tabaq borek because they are presented on a plate. Noodles and beans are often served together in easy but satisfying dishes, like Lacşa (see page 126).

Whether old or modern, a traditional Tatar house has an outdoor clay oven called a *pirim*. With the unbearably hot summers of Dobrogea, this is ideal for baking bread and making all the traditional specialities. Everyday bread is unleavened *pazlamaş*, made only with water and flour, and cooked outdoors on a hot flat iron, while *qalaqai* is a round, leavened bread, which during spring festivities is rolled down a slope like a wheel. On baking days, people slide trays of pies and pastries in with the bread to make the most of the heat in the *pirim*. One of these pies is *Kubete*, the most traditional meat pie (see page 206), which in Spring used to be made with lamb intestines, washed and chopped to look like minced meat.

Sweets were not part of the traditional nomadic Tatar cuisine, maybe just dried fruit. Today, Tatar desserts are influenced by Turkish baklavas, sweet pastries, and cakes in Romanian style. People will also make you an excellent Turkish coffee, even though drinking tea is more evocative of their life in the steppe than coffee. In some Tatar homes, I found ornate samovar sets displayed in the living room as decorations.

On the Golden Horde

It is perhaps difficult to accept the idea of Tatars looking for refuge in foreign lands when we usually associate them with the merciless East Asian military force that once reached as far as Hungary and Croatia.

Having started in the 12th century in today's Mongolia and under the leadership of the charismatic Chinggis Khan, the Mongols united all nomadic tribes found in their way under the name of Tatars. When the Empire split, its whole western area, from the Carpathian mountains and the northern shores of the Black Sea to Siberia and Iran formed the Golden Horde. The rulers were descendants of Chinggis Khan but independent from the Mongol Court and converted to Islam in the 14th century.

'From these vast lands,' historian Marie Favereau says in her book, *The Horde*, 'they maintained and grew the most extensive exchange of people, goods and ideas in the premodern world. They shaped the politics of Russia and of Central Asia and firmly anchored Islam in the Caucasus and Eastern Europe.'

The key aspect of their rule was to guarantee peace and consensus. They made travelling on the Silk Road and all trade routes safe, invested in an economic exchange that brought merchants from Egypt and Venice to as far as China, and invited diplomatic convoys, religious ambassadors, travellers and writers to be part of this flourishing global world. Their Qurultay election system acted like a Parliament and influenced many political systems in Eurasia. Another remarkable legacy was the ingenious postal system called Örtöö, based on an impressive network of relay posts.

They ruled without being visible, allowing people to elect their own leaders and make their own decisions as long as they paid their taxes. Even the tax collectors were local people. This is how the Rus tribes, Russians today, rose to power when they started to collect the tribute on behalf of the Horde.

The Russian Takeover

Historian Thomas T. Allsen, in his momentous work *Mongol Imperialism*, talks about the Russians trying to legitimise their new Empire by taking over and absorbing the legacy of the Horde. From this moment onwards, the weakened Horde split and the rest of the Tatars were conquered and forced to convert from Sunni Islam to Orthodox Christianity. Centuries later, Catherine the Great annexed the last standing Crimean

Khanate in 1783. Constantly targeted with persecution and reprisals, Tatars had to find refuge in the lands of the Ottoman Empire, including Dobrogea.

The Bolsheviks banned the Muslim faith and suppressed the Tatar language, Stalin deported and killed them, and Khrushchev gave Crimea to Ukraine in 1954 as part of the Russian Federation.

After the fall of the Soviet regime, Crimea failed to claim its independence and remained for a few years as part of Ukraine just to be annexed again by Putin to Russia. A report by Amnesty International in 2021 says, 'The international community may have few tools to address the underlying politics, but it must speak up for those being bullied and harassed into silence,' referring to the sudden disappearance of Tatars from homes and to the abusive imprisonment of dissidents.

This chapter features meat main courses, from the celebratory lamb stew with spring onions to braised chicken with broad (fava) beans, meat pie, and slow-cooked beef in a 'haiduc' style.

Pui la Cuptor cu Bob, Lăptuci și Cicoare

POT-ROASTED CHICKEN WITH BRAISED BROAD BEANS, LETTUCE AND WILD CHICORY

This is a light chicken recipe, which can be a summer alternative to your weekend roast. It also brings together ingredients that are now seeing a comeback in Romanian culinary conversations: broad (fava) beans and chicory (endive). There are many types of chicory, including a wild variety I saw in my journey through Oltenia and Muntenia, southern Romania, adorning the sides of the roads. Their leaves and blue flowers are edible and good in salads. But for practical reasons, I'll use a type of chicory that resembles dandelion or rocket (arugula), which is far easier to find.

Serves 4

oil, for cooking
1.5 kg (3 lb 5 oz) whole chicken
100 ml (3½ fl oz/scant ½ cup)
  dry white wine
400 ml (13 fl oz/generous
  1½ cups) chicken stock
2 medium brown onions, peeled
  and quartered
4 medium garlic cloves
2 thin rosemary sprigs
3–4 small thyme sprigs
250 g (9 oz) broad (fava) beans,
  frozen or fresh, shelled
2 romaine lettuce hearts,
  trimmed and cut into
  wide ribbons
100 g (3½ oz) chicory (endive),
  puntarelle or rocket
  (arugula) leaves
salt and freshly ground
  black pepper

To Serve

4 medium potatoes, washed
50 g (2 oz) unsalted butter
50 g (2 oz/scant ¼ cup)
  crème fraîche
1 teaspoon salt

Use a large enough casserole dish with a lid, approximately 23 cm (9 in) in diameter and 10cm (4 in) deep, to accommodate the chicken plus the extra ingredients. Preheat the oven to 160°C fan (310°F/gas 2).

Heat a thin layer of oil on the base of a casserole dish. Brown the chicken on all sides to get a bit of colour, then turn it breast side up, and add the wine, stock, onions, garlic and herbs. Put the lid on and place the dish in the oven for 1 hour 20 minutes.

After an hour, dice the potatoes, leaving the skin on. Place them in a deep pan, cover with water, bring to the boil and cook for 20 minutes until soft. Drain and return to the pan over a low heat, allowing some of the moisture to evaporate. Add the butter, crème fraîche and salt, and mash everything together. Cover the pan and keep warm until you are ready to serve.

Remove the chicken carefully to a plate or a chopping board and wrap it in kitchen foil. Add the broad beans, lettuce hearts and chicory (or rocket) to the stock in the pan and place it back in the oven, uncovered, for 10 minutes. Taste and adjust the seasoning.

(Alternatively, you can do this last step on the stove over a low heat but be careful because the casserole dish is hot, so use oven gloves to touch the lid and the handles.)

Carve the chicken and serve with the braised beans and leaves with generous spoonfuls of the stock over the mashed potatoes.

Stufat de Miel cu Lipie

LAMB AND SPRING ONION STEW
WITH FLATBREADS

Stufat is a popular lamb dish that Romanians prepare during Easter. Lamb is usually associated with this holiday, and every part of the animal is used to avoid wasting anything. These dishes are packed with flavour and are combined with seasonal plants and vegetables to celebrate youth, renewal and everything green. Traditionally, *stufat* is made using only the long green tops of spring onions (scallions) and garlic, which can also be braided to decorate the stew. I serve the dish with lipie, a traditional unleavened daily bread made with only flour and water. I add a little oil for texture.

Serves 4

Heat a thin layer of oil on the base of a large sauté pan and cook the lamb over a high heat for 5 minutes, browning on all sides. Remove to a plate. Add another splash of oil, reduce the heat to medium and fry the onions with a pinch of salt for 8–10 minutes until they caramelise. Stir occasionally so they don't burn, or add a drop of water. Add the garlic towards the end and fry briefly. Pour in the wine and allow the alcohol to evaporate, then return the lamb to the pan. Stir in the stock, cover the pan and simmer over a medium–low heat for 40 minutes until the lamb is tender.

While the lamb is cooking, mix the flatbread ingredients in a bowl and knead briefly to a smooth dough. Cover and leave until you are ready to cook.

Roughly chop the spring onions, including the green tops, spinach, chard and chives, and add to the stew pan. Combine well, cover and simmer for 5 minutes. Pour in the lemon juice, then taste and adjust the seasoning. Keep over a very low heat while you are grilling (broiling) the breads.

Divide the flatbread dough into 4 balls and roll each out to an 18 cm (7 in) circle. Heat a cast-iron or non-stick frying pan (skillet) and add enough oil to cover the base in a very thin layer. Cook each flatbread for 2–3 minutes on each side. As soon as each bread is ready, slide onto a plate lined with paper towel and covered with a plastic bag, to keep them soft.

Serve the stew immediately, scattering extra chopped chives on top, with the flatbreads and some lemon wedges on the side.

For the Stew

sunflower oil, for frying
500 g (1 lb 2 oz) diced lamb or boneless leg cut into chunks
2 medium brown onions, sliced
4 medium garlic cloves, chopped
25 ml (scant 2 tablespoons) white wine
200 ml (7 fl oz/scant 1 cup) vegetable stock
4 medium spring onions (scallions), ideally with long green tops (plus optional extra to garnish)
200 g (7 oz) spinach
200 g (7 oz) chard
20 g (¾ oz) chives, plus extra to garnish
juice of 1 large lemon, plus extra lemon wedges to serve
salt and freshly ground black pepper

For the Flatbreads

250 g (9 oz/2 cups) plain (all-purpose) flour
5 g (¼ oz) salt
35 ml (generous 2 tablespoons) sunflower or olive oil, plus extra for cooking
125 ml (4 fl oz/½ cup) water

Note

If you decide to go traditional, reserve a few spring onion green tops or chives and braid them in three strands or twist together in pairs, tying them in a small loop.

Varză cu Cârnați

SAUERKRAUT WITH PORK SAUSAGES

This is a simple dish that delivers big flavours. In Romania, people preserve cooked meat and sausages in a pot filled with rendered fat, called *la garniță*. It's considered a delicacy and is often used in stews or spread directly on bread. This method of preservation tenderises the meat and intensifies the flavours much like a confit. In the UK, when I don't have access to this ingredient, I use high-quality semi-cured or cured sausages that I cook slowly in oil to bring back some moisture. While not the same, fresh sausages can also be used in this dish.

Serves 4

sunflower oil, for frying
4 medium sausages, fresh
    or semi-cured
1 medium brown onion, sliced
a pinch of salt
500 g (1 lb 2 oz) sauerkraut
400 g (14 oz) tinned
    chopped tomatoes
1 teaspoon paprika
freshly ground black pepper

Drizzle the base of a large frying pan (skillet) with oil and heat. Turn the heat to medium and cook the sausages, turning them often to avoid sticking and burning. If you are using cured sausages, cook them over a medium–low heat for 5–6 minutes. Then, transfer the sausages to a plate and set aside.

Add the onion and a pinch of salt to the pan and cook over a medium heat until soft and slightly caramelised. Stir in the sauerkraut and fry for 5 minutes, then add the chopped tomatoes and paprika. Cook for 15 minutes and adjust the heat if the pan gets too hot.

Cut the sausages into 2–3 cm (¾–1 in) chunks and add them back to the pan, allowing them to warm through.

Serve immediately with bread, cornmeal bread or polenta, or boiled burghul wheat dotted with small pieces of butter.

Plăcintă cu Carne

TATAR KUBETE BEEF PIE

Kubete is a Tatar dish from Dobrogea, that is traditionally baked as a pie in round pans and cut into wedges. However, bakeries and even restaurants have opted for a more portable shape, selling it as filo triangles. Either way, the pie is served cold and without any side dishes, although you can add a fruit *compot* in the spirit of Tatar cuisine, or a potato salad (such as the one on page 88) in the spirit of Western cuisine.

Serves 4

50 ml (1¾ fl oz/3 tablespoons) sunflower oil
6 sheets of filo pastry, 50 x 30 cm (20 x 12 in) (wrap the rest in cling film/ plastic wrap, put back in the packet, keep in the refrigerator and use within a week)
2 teaspoons sesame seeds

For the Filling

sunflower oil, for frying
3 large onions, sliced
500 g (1 lb 2 oz) minced (ground) beef
1 teaspoon salt
2 teaspoons sweet paprika (*boia dulce*)
1 medium egg
1 tablespoon chopped parsley

Start with the filling. Heat a thin layer of oil on the base of a large frying pan (skillet) over a medium heat. Add the onions with a pinch of salt and cook until soft, around 8 minutes. Stir in the beef and salt, and cook until you can't see any pink patches and the meat is a light brown colour. There shouldn't be too much juice left in the pan either. If there is, cook it for a few more minutes. Allow to cool for 20 minutes, then stir in the paprika, egg and parsley.

Meanwhile, preheat the oven to 180°C fan (350°F/gas 4).

Brush a 22 cm (8½ in) pie dish with a little of the oil. Open the filo pastry sheets and cover them with a damp dish towel, which will keep them soft. Work with one sheet at a time, while the others stay covered. Brush a sheet with oil and place it in the pie dish, allowing almost half of it to hang over the rim. Repeat with the other pastry sheets, arranging and overlapping them in a star pattern, so that the base and the edges of the dish are covered evenly.

Spoon the filling evenly into the middle of the dish and start to fold the overhanging pastry over it, brushing it with more oil. Tuck any corners in, then brush the top with the leftover oil and sprinkle with the sesame seeds.

Bake for 25 minutes on a lower shelf.

Remove from the oven and leave it to rest for 20 minutes before serving. It is not served hot, but warm or completely cold.

Tocăniță Haiducească

HAIDUC STEW

Haiduci were bands of guerrilla fighters and outlaws, some would say bandits, who were opposed to the rule of the Ottoman Empire. In countries like Serbia and Bulgaria, they were fighting for freedom, while in southern Romania, which never fully lost its independence, they were fighting for social justice. They remained in our collective memory as the Knights of Justice, protecting the poor from the wealthy. Anyone could have joined their groups, and in fact, the most famous Romanian *haiduc,* Iancu Jianu, had initially been a landlord, *moșier*. Their stories continue to be romanticised and their lives are seen as an example of unyielding beliefs, bold actions and authenticity. A dish that brings together so many bold ingredients can only be named after them.

Serves 4

sunflower oil, for frying
500 g (1 lb 2 oz) diced beef
250 g (9 oz) smoked lardons
350 ml (12 fl oz/scant 1½ cups)
    red wine
5 medium brown onions,
    thinly sliced
a pinch of salt
400 g (14 oz) tinned finely
    chopped tomatoes
2 bay leaves
4 Romanian *Pleșcoi* sausages
    or British farmhouse pork
    sausages, cooked
150 g (9 oz) mushrooms, sliced

Cover the base of a large 26–28 cm (10½–1 in) sauté pan or casserole dish with a thin layer of oil and heat well. Add the beef and lardons, brown for 5–8 minutes, then transfer to a dish and set aside. Pour 2 tablespoons of the red wine into the pan and scrape off all the caramelised bits left on the base. Pour the resulting juices over the meat.

Add another thin layer of oil to the pan and cook the onions with a good pinch of salt over a medium heat until soft, around 15 minutes. Stir in the chopped tomatoes and bring to the boil. Return the beef and lardons to the pan, add the bay leaves and the remaining wine, then cover, reduce the heat and simmer gently for 1 hour 20 minutes, or until the meat is meltingly tender. Stir or shake the pan from time to time and keep the heat on low, so the sauce doesn't catch on the base.

Cut the cooked sausages into 3 cm (1 in) pieces. Add them to the pan together with the mushrooms and cook for 15 more minutes.

Serve with mashed potatoes, buttery polenta or thick slices of bread. A bowl of assorted pickles is also good.

Pastramă de Miel cu Mămăligă

PASTRAMI LAMB CHOPS WITH POLENTA

Pastramă is the name of cured and air-dried mutton leg or shoulder, cut into strips, then grilled or fried. It is served with polenta and garlic sauce, which is usually good for cutting through the richness of the meat. The traditional *pastramă* flavours are fenugreek, garlic, paprika and winter savory, and I'm taking inspiration from them to make a sauce to serve with lamb chops, which is very close to the original flavours.

Serves 4

sunflower oil, for frying
4 lamb chops
salt and freshly ground
  black pepper

For the Sauce

20 g (¾ oz) garlic cloves,
  very thinly sliced
100 ml (3½ fl oz/scant ½ cup)
  white wine or cold water
25 ml (scant 2 tablespoons)
  olive oil
5 g (¼ oz) salt
1 tablespoon chopped parsley
2 teaspoons *cimbru* (summer
  savory), dried savory
  or thyme
2 teaspoons sweet
  or smoked paprika
1 teaspoon ground fenugreek
1 teaspoon ground cumin
½ teaspoon chilli powder
1 tablespoon white wine vinegar

To Serve

1 batch of *Mămăligă* Polenta
  (see page 15)

Make the sauce by mixing all the ingredients in a bowl. Set aside.

If you are serving the dish with *Mămăligă* Polenta, now is the time to prepare it. Keep it on a low heat and it will be ready by the time you cook the chops.

Heat a dash of oil in a frying pan (skillet) over a high heat. Rub some oil into the lamb chops and sprinkle with salt and pepper on both sides. Sear the chops fat-side down for 5 minutes until golden and rendered, then cook for 3 minutes on each side. Pour the *pastramă* sauce over the chops (this will spit a little but you can put a lid on right away and allow it to calm down), keep the heat on high and cook for a further 2 minutes.

Serve with polenta and spoonfuls of the sauce.

Note

If the sauce reduces too much, add a splash of water and return the pan to the heat for a few seconds.

Pilaf cu Pui

CHICKEN PILAF WITH POTATOES AND GARLIC COURGETTES

A pilaf is one of the most popular dishes in Romania, a fantastic combination of any ingredients we have at hand, cooked together with rice: chicken pilaf, vegetable pilaf and even fruit pilaf. The rice is cooked in plenty of stock, and stewed gently in a covered pot until it reaches a creamy yet runny consistency.

Serves 4–6

35 ml (generous 2 tablespoons) sunflower oil
4 medium bone-in, skin-on chicken thighs
1 large brown onion, finely sliced
300 g (10½ oz) potatoes, cut into thick chunks
1 tablespoon white wine vinegar
250 g (9 oz/1¼ cups) long-grain white rice
1 litre (34 fl oz/4½ cups) vegetable or chicken stock
¼ teaspoon freshly ground black pepper
1 medium courgette (zucchini)
2 large garlic cloves
1 teaspoon chopped marjoram, fresh or dried
salt

To Serve

good olive oil
lemon wedges
tomato salad

Preheat the oven to 170°C fan (325°F/gas 3).

Use a 23–24 cm (9–9½ in), 12 cm (5 in) deep casserole dish with a lid (otherwise, cooking times may differ).

Cover its base with the oil and heat well. Sprinkle the chicken with salt generously, and fry the thighs in one layer for 15 minutes, turning often. Keep the heat on medium so they don't burn, then transfer the cooked chicken to a plate.

Fry the onion with a good pinch of salt in the remaining oil over a medium heat for 8 minutes. Add the potatoes, combine well and fry for another 3 minutes, then add the vinegar and scrape the base of the pan with a spatula to remove all those caramelised bits.

Place the chicken thighs on top of the potatoes in one layer, then scatter the rice on top and add the stock. Taste the stock to make sure it's salty enough; if not, add more to the dish. The secret to a good pilaf is using a generous amount of salt. Add the black pepper, then cover and cook in the oven for 25 minutes. It will make a rather loose pilaf. Alternatively, cook it until the stock is completely absorbed.

Meanwhile, grate the courgette and garlic together and mix with the marjoram. When the rice is cooked, spread this mixture on top, put the lid back on and leave the pan to sit for 5 minutes out of the oven.

Serve immediately with a drizzle of your best olive oil, wedges of lemon to squeeze on top and a tomato salad.

A LAND

OF FRUIT
AND NUTS

A Blended Present: Turkish Communities

'I'm half Tatar and half Turkish with some Armenian blood too, and my husband, Ecrem, is Turkish from Ada Kaleh,' says Filiz Ismail, President of the Turkish Women Association, when I met her in Constanța. This is the story of many people in Dobrogea, they come from mixed ethnic families, and it is a wonderful thing to see this blended past reflected in day-to-day life. If, during the Communist regime, ethnic groups were muted, living somehow under the radar, today they are embraced wholeheartedly.

Turkish people in Romania observe their religious traditions, form political unions, and are supported by the government with grants to promote their culture, write in and speak their own language. Most importantly, they keep restaurants and serve traditional dishes, preserving their past through food.

In Constanța, a city port with the largest Turkish community in the country, I loved hearing the Turkish language spoken in shops or on the street. I loved seeing how people greeted each other according to the custom with a hand on their heart. In the Old Town, its narrow lanes lined with little shops, bakeries and cafés take you to Kral Camii Mosque, called Geamia Regelui, The King's Mosque. It's one of the few mosques in the world to be named after a Christian king. Its construction was ordered in 1910 by King Carol I of Romania, a member of the German House of Hohenzollern, who wanted to strengthen the bond between the people of these two religions. To this day, it speaks of the ethnic tolerance that has existed in Dobrogea for centuries.

What impressed me the most was to see the role played by Turkish women in their community. Organised in associations across Dobrogea (and the country), they get together regularly to discuss different customs, learn from one another and incorporate old traditions into the practicalities of modern life. Every year, they plan festivals and attend culinary events, feasts where everyone is welcome, contributing to the community spirit in the city.

The Influence of Turkish Cuisine in the Danube Lands

You only need to pick up a restaurant menu in Romania or anywhere along the Danube to recognise so many Turkish dishes, even if the names are slightly misleading. It is obvious that we share a culinary history influenced by centuries of trade, Turkish political interference and military presence. In Romania, the first groups came in peace in 1262, following the dervish Baba Sari Saltik to Babadag, where we have the country's oldest mosque and a place of pilgrimage. Later, the Ottomans came to rule. Although we never completely lost our independence, we were a vassal state, and people were not displaced or forced to convert to Islam.

Ottoman cuisine itself was a succession and fusion of culinary traditions accumulated from the nomadic tribes of Central Asia and the royal cuisines of Persia and Byzantium. The Empire spent time refining dishes, whose names were later made popular throughout all its lands and further afield.

Culinary Infidelities

As author Anya von Bremzen said in her book *National Dish*: 'Taste is not only deeply subjective but also associative. [...] Names of foods influence flavour perception [...] and conjure up different associations and cultural memories.' In Romania, some names are still testimony of the Ottoman-imposed rule over the country, even if the recipes are different. However, a Romanian *ciorbă* is never going to be the same as a Turkish *çorbası*, for those exact cultural and family memories Anya talks about.

Here are a few Romanian dishes with a Turkish name:

*Ciorb*ă in Romania is a sour soup, one of the everyday, essential meals served even at festivities (see more on page 115). It usually contains vegetables, meat, herbs and foraged plants, being different from the Turkish dish *çorbası* by not using rice or burghul and by having a thin consistency. The old name was *zeamă*, broth, which is considered our national dish.

Iahnie comes from the Persian *yakhni*, and was initially a meat ragout. In Romania, it is a fantastic vegetarian dish made with slow-cooked white beans. It is often served for Lent, however on feast days it can benefit from a topping of grilled (broiled) sausage or a slow-cooked ham hock (see page 142).

Ghiveci is a stew named after the Turkish *güveç*, an earthenware casserole in which it was cooked. In Romania, we associate it with a mix of vegetables, whatever is in season, slow-cooked without meat, in the oven (see the recipe on page 156). If we add meat, we call it *ghiveci cu carne*.

Musaca is another dish in Romania that hails from Turkish and Medieval Arab cuisine. Dr Özge Samancı says in her book *La Cuisine d'Istanbul au XIXe Siècle* that both dolma and mussakka dishes called for stuffed, rolled vegetables or leaves, the difference being that the first was cooked on the stove, and the latter in the oven. Later, it developed into the layered dish we associate with Greece today (see the fish version on page 182).

Sarma is so popular in Romania that we consider it one of our national dishes, 'national' meaning what our nation eats across the country. There are many culinary conversations in Romania regarding the rolled leaves, *sarmale*, as to whether the technique was known to us before we imported the word, and the answer is yes (see page 161).

Ciulama comes from *cullamasi*, meaning a pounded vegetable sauce or coating. Musa Dağdeviren gives two recipes in his momentous *The Turkish Cookbook* with breaded or poached chicken and pounded boiled vegetables. In Romania, *ciulama* is a white sauce often made by frying flour in butter or thickening sour cream with flour (see the recipe on page 140).

Pilaf is a wonderfully versatile rice dish, which in Ottoman cuisine is used as a bed for resting and serving grilled meats. In Romania, it has the comfort of a risotto made with long-grain rice (see recipes on pages 210 and 186).

Chiftea, the Turkish kofte, is made with minced (ground) pork, and they resemble meat patties. *Pastramă* cured beef is disputed between the Armenians, who call it *basturma*, and the Turkish. Romanians prepare it with mutton and serve it grilled with polenta and garlic sauce.

When it comes to desserts, we share our love for Baklava (see page 221), *Cataif* (page 232), *caimac* (clotted cream), *şerbet* (fruit butter), *saraili* (crinkled filo and walnut pastries), and – of course – the drink that conquered the world: *cafea* (coffee). This chapter showcases easy-to-make desserts from puddings to roulades and baklavas to fresh fruit served with custard or curd cheese.

Budincă de Griș

SEMOLINA MILK SOUFFLÉ

This is a feather-like dessert traditional throughout the Balkans and north of the Danube in countries that were once part of the Austrian Empire. In Romania it is called *budincă*, as in 'pudding', but in many other countries it is *koch* or *koh*, retaining its Austrian roots. The recipe is similar to a soufflé and unusual in the way you pour milk over it when it's out of the oven. It is served with milk or fruit sauce or left plain.

Serves 4

butter, for greasing
granulated sugar, for coating
4 medium eggs, separated
100 g (3½ oz/scant ½ cup)
    caster (superfine) sugar
100 g (3½ oz/generous ¾ cup)
    fine semolina
1 teaspoon lemon zest
2 tablespoons rum
50 g (2 oz) fresh raspberries,
    halved, plus extra to serve

To Serve

600 ml (20 fl oz/2½ cups) milk
80 g (3 oz/⅓ cup) caster sugar
2 teaspoons vanilla paste

Thoroughly butter a 23 cm (9 in) ceramic baking/pie dish, then sprinkle the base and sides with granulated sugar. Preheat the oven to 180°C fan (350°F/gas 4).

Beat the egg yolks with half of the caster sugar until fluffy and pale, then mix in the semolina, lemon zest and rum. Whisk the egg whites to soft peaks, then add the rest of the sugar and whisk to stiff peaks. Fold them gently into the semolina mixture. Using a serving spoon, place large dollops of the mixture in the prepared dish, and place the halved raspberries on top.

Bake on a lower shelf for 10 minutes, then reduce the heat to 160°C (310°F/gas 2) and cook for another 10 minutes, or until the top turns golden brown. Test with a wooden cocktail stick (toothpick) to see if it comes out clean.

Meanwhile, heat the milk and sugar in a pan, adding the vanilla after the sugar has dissolved. Keep the pan warm, and right after you take the pudding out of the oven, pour half of the warm milk over the pudding and around the edges. Allow the milk to be absorbed for 2–3 minutes, then serve with fresh raspberries and the rest of the milk poured around each portion.

Baclava de Tulcea

TULCEA BAKLAVA

This is a fascinating baklava from the Turkish and Tatar communities in Tulcea, Dobrogea. The filo pastry is made from scratch and every baklava triangle is shaped by hand. The recipe that follows is an achievable version with store-bought filo pastry, trying to replicate the traditional folding technique.

Makes 18 small pieces

For the Syrup

300 ml (10 fl oz/1¼ cups) water
200 g (7 oz/scant 1 cup) caster (superfine) sugar
2 medium lemons: 1 juiced; 1 thinly sliced

For the Baklava

12 standard filo pastry sheets
75 ml (2½ fl oz/5 tablespoons) melted unsalted butter
150 g (5 oz) walnuts, roughly chopped

Make the syrup by bringing all the ingredients to the boil in a deep, 16 cm (6¼ in) pan. Turn the heat to medium-high and boil for 10 minutes until the liquid starts to thicken.

Preheat the oven to 180°C fan (350°F/gas 4). Line a large baking pan or sheet, 32 x 22 cm (13 x 8½ in) or larger, with baking parchment.

Keep the filo sheets under a damp dish towel and work with one at a time. Keeping the long side closest to you, brush with butter, then place a second filo sheet on top and brush with butter. Divide vertically into three equal strips. Fold the shorter sides of the strips towards the middle and adjust them to look like a square. Now fold the square in half from top to bottom, and again from left to right.

Brush the top with a small amount of butter after each fold. Place a small amount of chopped walnuts in the middle, then fold diagonally to make a triangle. You don't need to press on the layers or seal the triangle.

Repeat with another strip of pastry, then place both triangles in the lined pan or baking sheet, back to back. Repeat with the rest of the filo sheets and you will end up with 18 small baklavas.

Bake for 20 minutes. Remove from the oven and transfer them immediately to a plate in a single layer. Spoon over the syrup, including the lemon slices. Allow to cool and serve.

Prăjitură cu Mere

APPLE ROULADE WITH VANILLA CUSTARD

This is the rolled version of the Romanian layered apple pie. The roulade is not a sponge but a yeasted dough, easy to work with and remarkably soft. The filling is tangy and not too sweet, allowing the natural flavour of apples to come through. Although it is usually served as a snack, I like to add a warm vanilla custard, bringing it closer to a pudding. It is not traditional but very good.

Serves 4–6

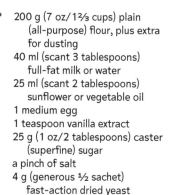

200 g (7 oz/1⅔ cups) plain
   (all-purpose) flour, plus extra
   for dusting
40 ml (scant 3 tablespoons)
   full-fat milk or water
25 ml (scant 2 tablespoons)
   sunflower or vegetable oil
1 medium egg
1 teaspoon vanilla extract
25 g (1 oz/2 tablespoons) caster
   (superfine) sugar
a pinch of salt
4 g (generous ½ sachet)
   fast-action dried yeast

For the Filling

600 g (1 lb 5 oz) Braeburn
   apples, grated
25 g (1 oz/2 tablespoons) caster
   (superfine) sugar
zest and juice of 1 large lemon
1 teaspoon vanilla extract

To Serve

1 teaspoon icing
   (powdered) sugar
1 teaspoon ground cinnamon
500 ml (17 fl oz/2 cups) vanilla
   custard, warm

First, make the dough by combining all the ingredients in a bowl. Knead briefly, cover and leave to to rest for 30 minutes.

Meanwhile, cook the apples with the sugar, lemon zest and juice in a sauté pan over a medium–high heat. When the juices are reduced and the apples start to caramelise, turn the heat off, add the vanilla and leave to cool.

Preheat the oven to 170°C fan (325°F/gas 3). Line a large baking sheet with baking parchment.

Flour your work surface and the dough generously and roll the dough out to a 35 x 45 cm (14 x 18 in) rectangle. Keep flouring while you roll it to avoid sticking. Spread the apples evenly on top, leaving a 1 cm (½ in) margin on the left and right short sides. Roll it into a log, place your hand underneath and lift it onto the baking sheet.

Bake for 30–35 minutes until golden on top. It might split along the sides, but that's okay.

Remove from the oven and cover with a clean dish towel for 15 minutes. I like to serve it slightly warm, dusted with a mix of icing sugar and cinnamon on top, with some vanilla custard. It keeps well for another day or two.

Pepene cu Brânză Dulce

CURD CHEESE WITH WATERMELON AND SESAME SEEDS

This recipe is my own, taking inspiration from Romanians' love for watermelons. There is an area near the Danube where the soil is sandy and perfect for growing watermelons, and the farmers have already developed a brand of their own: *Dulce de Dăbuleni*. The watermelons are so famous that it is even reported in the news when the season opens. The recipe combines ingredients that are prominent in our cuisine throughout all ethnic communities. It is a refreshing dessert, much needed on a hot summer's evening.

Serves 4

25 g (1 oz) sesame seeds
200 g (7 oz) *brânză de vaci*, curd cheese (alternatively, use 300 g/10½ oz ricotta and omit the yoghurt)
100 g (3½ oz/generous ⅓ cup) thick, plain yoghurt
1 tablespoon runny honey, plus extra to drizzle
1 teaspoon rose water (optional)
50 g (2 oz/generous ¼ cup) diced crystallised (candied) orange peel, plus extra to decorate
½ medium watermelon

Toast the sesame seeds in a dry pan over a medium–low heat. Keep an eye on them, because they can burn in a second. Transfer to a plate and set aside.

Mix all the ingredients, apart from the watermelon, in a bowl, then divide among four dessert plates.

Cut the watermelon into 4 slices, then place them next to the curd cheese. Drizzle with more honey and sprinkle with the sesame seeds and extra crystallised peel.

Sugiuc

ADA KALEH PEKMEZ-ROASTED WALNUTS

200 g (7 oz) walnut halves
50 g (2 oz) *pekmez*
(grape molasses)
½ teaspoon salt, or to taste

The island of Ada Kaleh stood in the middle of the Danube, near the town of Orşova. It was one of the last Ottoman strongholds at the northern edge of their empire, its name meaning 'the castle island'. For hundreds of years, it remained a time capsule of all Ottoman customs and traditions. Tourists and traders travelling by boat to Istanbul would stop to enjoy the famous Ada Kaleh coffee and sweets soaked in syrup, as a prelude to many delicacies that awaited them at their destination. However, in 1970, the fate of the island was sealed forever, when the Romanian and Serbian authorities decided to construct the Iron Gates Hydroelectric Dam and make the Danube more navigable. Men, women and children stood powerless on the riverbank, watching their island and homes being submerged. People were dispersed to other Turkish ethnic communities in Dobrogea or their families in Turkey. Meeting with some of them, I was shocked to realise how recent this event still felt and how nostalgia and the burden of loss mixed in their voices.

Ecrem Ismail spent his childhood on the island, and he remembered the fruit orchards, the musmula medlar trees, the wild olive trees and his mum's rose petal jam. Scented roses and jasmine climbed over ornate archways, and the lanes were adorned with magnolias. The recipe that follows is a sweet reminder of those times and of one of the most famous confectioneries: *sugiuc*. Traditionally, walnut halves were stacked onto a long string, resembling a thin sausage, and dipped in a thick mixture of grape molasses, called *pekmez*, and flour. Here is a simplified recipe that evokes the original flavours.

Makes 200 g (7 oz)

Preheat the oven to 180°C fan (350°F/gas 4). Line a baking sheet with baking parchment.

In a bowl, mix the walnuts with the pekmez and salt, then spread them in one layer on the baking sheet and roast on the middle shelf of the oven for 5–8 minutes until the pekmez starts to caramelise.

Remove from the oven and leave the walnuts to cool on the sheet. Some will be gooey, others crunchy. Taste and add more salt if you like. Serve as a snack.

Prăjitură cu Nucă

WALNUT AND FENNEL SEED CAKE WITH CLOTTED CREAM AND POACHED QUINCE

We are very fond of walnuts and quince in Romania, and quince trees seem to be in every single garden in the south, especially in Dobrogea. They have the perfect climate here, and people make compôtes for the winter, which are canned poached quince, or use them in stews with rice and even make brandy. I played with these ingredients to make a light cake to capture Dobrogea's autumnal (fall) flavours. Fennel also grows in the fields and in gardens, having originally been brought to these ancient lands by the Romans.

Makes a 900 g (2 lb) loaf cake

Preheat the oven to 160°C fan (310°F/gas 2). Grease and line a 900 g (2 lb) loaf pan.

Using an electric mixer, whisk the egg whites to soft peaks, then add the light brown sugar and whisk for 1 minute on high speed. Add the egg yolks one at a time, then the oil and sour cream, incorporating well after each addition. Flavour with rum and vanilla.

In a separate bowl, mix the flour with the baking powder and salt, then sift over the egg mixture, folding a couple of times with a large metal spoon. Fold in the walnuts and fennel seeds, making sure there are no dry patches.

Pour the batter into the loaf pan and bake for 30 minutes, or until a cocktail stick (toothpick) inserted in the middle of the cake comes out clean. Turn out of the pan onto a cooling rack.

Meanwhile, make the poached quince. Mix the water, caster sugar, honey, lemon zest and juice, herb sprigs and vanilla in a large pan and bring to the boil. Quarter the quince and remove the cores. Cut each quarter into two. Place the slices in the pan as you go along, then reduce the heat to low and simmer gently for 15 minutes, or until soft. Turn the heat off and leave to cool.

Slice the cake and dust it with icing sugar. Serve with the quince slices on the side, topped with a spoonful of clotted cream. Drizzle some of the poaching liquid around each slice.

For the Cake

65 ml (2 fl oz/¼ cup) sunflower oil, plus extra for greasing
3 medium eggs, separated
50 g (2 oz/generous ¼ cup) light brown sugar
65 g (2¼ oz/¼ cup) sour cream
25 ml (scant 2 tablespoons) rum or any brandy
1 teaspoon vanilla extract or paste
100 g (3½ oz/generous ¾ cup) plain (all-purpose) flour
10 g (½ oz/2 teaspoons) baking powder
a pinch of salt
120 g (4 oz) walnuts, finely chopped
5 g (1 teaspoon) dried fennel seeds

For the Poached Quince

500 ml (17 fl oz/2 cups) water
80 g (3 oz/⅓ cup) caster (superfine) sugar
25 ml (scant 2 tablespoons) runny honey (not raw)
zest and juice of 1 medium lemon
4–5 thyme sprigs
3 rosemary sprigs
1 tablespoon dried camomile (optional)
1 vanilla pod (bean), split, or 2 teaspoons vanilla extract
2 medium quince

To Serve

icing (powdered) sugar, for dusting
200 g (7 oz/generous ¾ cup) clotted cream or extra thick double (heavy) cream

Cataif cu Griș

SEMOLINA CATAIF WITH CHERRY JAM AND PISTACHIOS

I first saw this dessert at a Turkish food event. All the women's associations in the country cooked and baked their own regional dishes to be sampled by the guests and public. This dessert was from the capital, Bucharest. It had been baked in a rectangular tray and cut into small pieces, then served with a small confit cherry on top and a scattering of chopped pistachios. I tried it at home and it's the perfect dish for when you have guests. You can make it hours in advance and serve chilled. I find it easier to layer it in individual ramekins or large coffee cups than to assemble it in a tray.

Serves 4–6

Make the syrup by bringing the water and sugar to the boil. Keep the pan over a high heat and cook for 8–10 minutes until the syrup starts to thicken. Add the lemon juice and rose water, bring to the boil again, then turn off the heat and set aside.

Preheat the oven to 180°C fan (350°F/gas 4).

Line a baking sheet or tray large enough to accommodate the pastry in a thin layer.

In a bowl, separate the pastry strands so they don't clump together, pour the melted butter over them and coat the strands in butter as thoroughly as possible. Transfer to the baking sheet and bake for 10–15 minutes until the pastry looks golden brown. Remove from the oven and use a spoon to evenly drizzle the syrup on top. Set aside.

Make the filling by bringing the milk and sugar to the boil. Reduce the heat to low and sprinkle over the semolina, using a whisk to disperse it in the milk. Cook over a low heat for a few minutes, stirring often, until it thickens, then set aside for 10 minutes. Whisk in the egg yolks really quickly, then set aside.

Place a layer of pastry in the base of four or six 12 cm (5 in) dessert bowls. Spoon over some of the semolina filling, then add another layer of pastry, a teaspoon of cherry jam and a sprinkling of pistachios. Serve immediately or chill in the refrigerator to serve cold.

For the Syrup

300 ml (10 fl oz/1¼ cups) water
150 g (5 oz/⅔ cup) caster (superfine) sugar
juice of 2 medium lemons
1 teaspoon rose water (optional)

For the Pastry

225 g (8 oz) kataifi pastry (found in Middle Eastern stores or online)
100 g (3½ oz) unsalted butter, melted

For the Filling

500 ml (17 fl oz/2 cups) full-fat milk
35 g (1¼ oz/2½ tablespoons) caster (superfine) sugar
125 g (4 oz/1 cup) semolina
2 medium egg yolks

To Decorate

150 g (5 oz/scant ½ cup) cherry jam (or more depending on your preference)
80 g (3 oz/scant ⅔ cup) chopped pistachios

Bucte cu Trei Haine

GERNÍK BUNS WITH POPPY SEEDS, CURD CHEESE AND JAM

Gerník is one of the Czech villages in Romania where the locals bake these 'buns with three jackets', referring to the three fillings that go in the middle. The buns are served for breakfast or as an easy pick-me-up in the afternoon with a cup of coffee. They are a snack rather than a pudding.

Makes 12 small buns

For the Dough

275 g (10 oz/2 ¼ cups) plain (all-purpose) flour, plus extra for dusting
40 g (1½ oz/3 tablespoons) caster (superfine) sugar
7 g (1 sachet) fast-action dried yeast
a pinch of salt
1 medium egg
25 ml (scant 2 tablespoons) sunflower oil
110 ml (3¾ fl oz/scant ½ cup) full-fat milk

For the Filling

120 g (4 oz) cottage cheese
1 medium egg yolk
20 g (¾ oz/1½ tablespoons) caster (superfine) sugar
zest of 1 small lemon
10 g (½ oz/1 tablespoon) poppy seeds, plus extra to decorate
120 g (4 oz/generous ⅓ cup) strawberry jam

To Glaze

1 medium egg yolk mixed with 1 tablespoon water

First, make the dough. Combine all the ingredients in a bowl, then knead for a few seconds until the dough is smooth. Cover the bowl and leave to prove for 45 minutes in a warm place.

Make the filling by mixing the cottage cheese with the egg yolk, sugar, lemon zest and poppy seeds. Set aside.

Divide the dough into 12 equal balls, around 40 g (1½ oz) each. Sprinkle your work surface with flour if necessary. Place on a large baking sheet, cover and leave for 15 minutes in a warm place.

Preheat the oven to 170°C fan (325°F/gas 3).

Dip a teaspoon in flour and make a well in the middle of each ball, pressing all the way down then around to form a disc with raised edges, 5.5 cm (2 ¼ in) in diameter. You can use the base of a small glass to make the initial well larger. Dip it in flour, so it doesn't stick, then stamp it into each dough ball. Brush with the egg wash all over, especially around the edges.

Place 1 teaspoon of the cheese mixture in the middle of each bun, followed by 1 teaspoon of jam and sprinkle some extra poppy seeds on top.

Bake on a lower shelf of the oven for 12–14 minutes until the edges are beautifully golden. Transfer to a cooling rack, then serve warm.

Note

You can use any other jam and even fresh fruit, such as thin slices of plums or apricots, or blueberries and blackcurrants.

Biscuiți Regele Carol

KING CAROL I CHOCOLATE BISCUITS

These biscuits were produced by Ludwig Josiek at his Pasta and Biscuit Factory in the Romanian Danube town of Galați. In 1900, it was the first steam-powered factory in the country, producing different pasta shapes, for which they won international awards, couscous and orzo. In the interwar period, the Czech owner decided to open a new section called 'French and English biscuits' and launched Carol chocolate biscuits, mirroring the fashion of chocolate treats in Western Europe. They were celebrating King Carol I of Hohenzollern, the monarchy that ruled Romania between 1866 and 1947.

The initial, beautifully crafted biscuit stamp can be seen in the local museum but there is no recipe on record. The factory was nationalised after WWII and renamed Danubiana, and what really ended its life was the period after the fall of the communist regime in 1989 when it became dilapidated and abandoned. The recipe is my best guess after reading an advertisement from those times: delicate vanilla-scented chocolate biscuits.

Makes 24 small, thin cookies

125 g (4 oz) unsalted
    butter, softened
120 g (4 oz/generous ½ cup)
    caster (superfine) sugar
1 medium egg
2 teaspoons orange
    blossom water
1 tablespoon vanilla extract
40 g (1½ oz/⅓ cup)
    cocoa (unsweetened
    chocolate) powder
180 g (6¼ oz/scant 1½ cups)
    plain (all-purpose) flour
½ teaspoon baking powder

Beat the butter with the sugar until creamy and almost white in colour. Beat in the egg, then add the orange blossom water and vanilla. Mix in the dry ingredients, using a spoon to incorporate everything well until you can't see any dry patches. The mixture is very sticky. Wrap it in a large piece of cling film (plastic wrap) and press it down into a disc. Put it in the freezer for 30 minutes. It still needs to be malleable after this.

Place the dough in between two sheets of baking parchment and roll it out to 5 mm (¼ in) thick. Peel off the sheet on top, then put it back and turn the dough over, peeling off the other sheet. If the dough looks too sticky, give it 5 more minutes in the freezer before cutting out a batch of 12 cookies with a 6 cm (2½ in) cookie cutter (crown shaped or regular). Place the cookies onto a lined baking sheet, spaced slightly apart, and return them to the freezer.

Preheat the oven to 160°C fan (310°F/gas 2).

Bake the cookies for 12 minutes, then remove them to a cooling rack.

Repeat with the rest of the dough until you use it all up, putting it in the freezer if it gets too sticky. Put the cookies in the freezer while the previous batch is baking.

They keep for 4–5 days in an airtight container and travel well, too. Perfect for gifts.

Căpșuni cu Șodou

STRAWBERRIES WITH ROSE WATER
CRÈME ANGLAISE

This is a very easy and refreshing dessert for when strawberries are in season. Rose water is an exquisite flavour that, in my opinion, makes any dessert tempting. The crème anglaise is more of an excuse to carry the flavours, and hence you can add your favourite combinations, from elderflower cordial or apple juice to any fruity liqueurs or even something stronger.

Serves 4

300 g (10½ oz)
   fresh strawberries
20 g (¾ oz) freshly chopped
   mint, plus extra to decorate
25 ml (scant 2 tablespoons)
   vodka or gin (optional)

For the Rose Water
Crème Anglaise

200 ml (7 fl oz/scant 1 cup)
   full-fat milk
3 egg yolks
25 g (1 oz/2 tablespoons)
   caster (superfine) sugar
2 teaspoons vanilla extract
2 teaspoons rose water

Slice or quarter the strawberries, place in a bowl and mix them with the mint and vodka. Set aside.

For the crème anglaise, warm the milk in a pan. It doesn't have to be boiling hot. In a bowl, whisk the egg yolks with the sugar briefly, then pour the warm milk over the mixture, whisking all the time. Return the mixture to the pan. Keep the heat on medium and whisk slowly until the crème thickens. This is a thin custard, so it has to have the consistency of single (light) cream. Remove from the heat and add the vanilla and rose water. Leave to cool at room temperature or chill it in the refrigerator.

When you are ready to serve, spoon some of the rose water crème anglaise into your serving dish, then top with strawberries.

A LAND OF

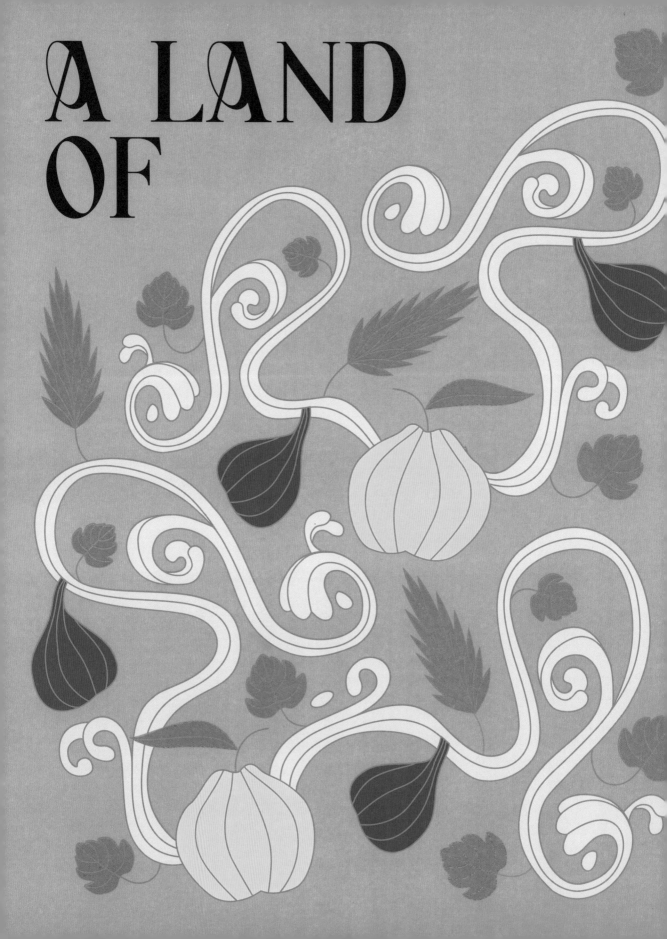

DELICACIES

Preserving the Lands of the Danube

As you read this, we have come to the end of our journey together. We have explored many lands along the Danube that were unknown to us at the beginning and learned about their stories.

For thousands of years, this mighty river has provided a route for trade and migration, while its lands have been a shelter and home for many communities.

Today, people living along the Danube, from its source in Germany to the delta in Romania, cherish and celebrate this strong bond through international events and projects. Some projects aim to preserve the natural beauty of the lands where they meet the river, and others encourage tourism through folk art and culinary festivals.

As you can sense throughout this book, the cuisine itself acts as a bridge between history and the present, and between nations and ethnic groups. It is this bridge that becomes the culinary identity of the Danube, that keeps its lands united and celebrates its people.

Thank you for being part of this journey, and let's celebrate with the fantastic fig jam, rum coffee, quince liqueur and millet drink that follow in this chapter.

Dulceață de Smochine

FIG CONFITURE

Svinița village, perched on top of cliffs overlooking the Danube, has the perfect climate for growing figs. Locals make a famous fig jam (trademarked!) and also brandy and liqueur, and celebrate the fig harvest every August in an annual festival. My recipe is a little different to the original, as I use jam sugar to make it quicker. The figs are cooked whole – you can either peel them before cooking, which is the method advised by my host Lina Dragotoiu, or leave them unpeeled, which my family prefer. This is a soft-set, runny sort of jam.

Makes 2 x 250 ml (8½ fl oz) jars

500 g (1 lb 2 oz) fresh figs
250 ml (8½ fl oz/1 cup) water
zest and juice of 1 large lemon
250 g (9 oz/generous
    1 cup) jam sugar with pectin

Top and tail the figs but keep them whole. Place them in a deep, 2 litre (68 fl oz/8½ cups) saucepan (about 18 cm/7 in in diameter) and cover with the measured water, adding the lemon zest and juice. Bring
to the boil, then cook over a medium-high heat for 20 minutes.

Add the sugar and shake the pan gently to help it dissolve. You can use a spatula, but be very gentle so as not to crush the figs. Cook for a further 25–30 minutes until the syrup thickens to the consistency of runny honey. Drizzle a little on a cold plate, wait for a few seconds and see if it sets to the right consistency.

Transfer to a bowl and store in the refrigerator for up to a week or decant into sterilised jars.

To sterilise the jars, I use the water bath method. Put a cloth on the base of a large pan and place the jars and the lids in the pan. Cover with water, bring to 80°C (175°F) and simmer for 20 minutes. When the jam is ready, remove the jars from the water, carefully pour in the hot jam right up to the brim and seal. They will keep for a couple of months. If you are planning to keep the jam for longer, return the filled jars to the pan, submerge them, bring back to 80°C (175°F) and simmer for 20 minutes. Remove and turn the jars upside down to cool on their lids.

Note

It's not traditional but you can also add mint or crushed aniseed or fennel seeds, almond or vanilla essence.

Suc de Muguri de Pin

SPRUCE BUD CORDIAL

In Romania, this is a well-known and popular cordial made from pine or spruce buds that are foraged in late spring. The tips of the branches are bright green and full of vitamin C; perfect for making cordials, pickling or infusing in vinegar, and even for making infused alcoholic drinks. Make sure you identify the tree correctly and also be mindful when you forage because the tips represent the new growth of the branches that year. It is better to take from several mature trees rather than very young ones.

Makes 500 ml (17 fl oz/2 cups)

600 ml (20 fl oz/2½ cups) water
300 g (10½ oz) pine
   or spruce buds
350 g (12 oz/1½ cups) caster
   (superfine) sugar
juice of 1 large lemon

Bring the water to the boil in a large pan, add the buds and simmer over a low heat for 30 minutes. Cover and allow to infuse for 24 hours.

Strain the liquid into a measuring jug and add 70g (2½ oz/ scant ⅓ cup) sugar for every 100 ml (3½ fl oz/scant ½ cup) of liquid. So, if you have 500 ml (17 fl oz/2 cups) liquid, add 350 g (12 oz/1½ cups) sugar.

Transfer back to the pan, add the lemon juice and bring to the boil again until the sugar dissolves. While it is still hot, pour into a sterilised bottle (see below) and seal. Store in the refrigerator and consume within a week.

Sterilise the bottle by submerging it in a saucepan of water lined with a cloth. Bring the water to around 80°C (175°F) and keep it at this temperature for 15 minutes.

To make the cordial last for up to 4 months, place the bottle up to its neck back in the water and keep it at 80°C (175°F) for 20 minutes.

Vinete Murate

PICKLED AUBERGINES WITH VEGETABLES

This quick aubergine (eggplant) pickle is inspired by
a recipe I was given by the Turkish community in Babadag,
Dobrogea. They use whole aubergines stuffed with vegetables
and preserved in large jars. It takes time and has many stages,
therefore I adapted it so we can use it in a couple of days.
The idea of 'fridge' pickles, meaning ones that don't need
maturing in the pantry for months, comes from Diana
Henry's clever *Salt Sugar Smoke* book.

Makes 1 x 1 litre (34 fl oz/4½ cups) jar or 2 smaller jars

In a large bowl, mix together the cabbage, red pepper and carrot,
then massage the salt into them. Set aside for at least 30 minutes
while you are preparing the other ingredients. By the time you
are ready to use it, the volume will have reduced and there will
be a lot of liquid at the bottom of the bowl. Add the parsley and
combine well.

Half-fill a large pan with water, add a generous amount
of salt and bring to the boil. Cut the aubergines in half lengthwise,
then into 1 cm (½ in) slices and drop them in the water. Blanch
over a medium heat until they start to soften in the middle.
Remove to a large plate lined with paper towel and leave until
they are cool enough to handle. Press them with more paper towel
to squeeze all the liquid out.

Sterilise your jar/s (see page 247). Meanwhile, make the
pickling brine by bringing all the ingredients to the boil in a small
pan, stirring to dissolve the salt. Keep the pan on a low heat.

Remove the sterilised jar/s from the water. Squeeze the liquid
out of the vegetables in the bowl, add a thin layer to the base
of the jar/s and press well. Pour in some pickling brine, then add
a layer of aubergine slices. Add a garlic clove and some green chilli.
Repeat this layering up to the rim of the jar/s and keep pressing
the layers to compress. Seal the jar/s and place on a little plate,
in case any extra liquid escapes, then refrigerate. The pickles will
be ready in 3 days.

1 small pointed sweetheart
  cabbage, shredded
1 medium red (bell)
  pepper, diced
1 medium carrot, grated
1 tablespoon salt, plus extra for
  salting the cooking water
30 g (1 oz) flat-leaf
  parsley, chopped
2 medium aubergines
  (eggplants)
2 medium garlic cloves, peeled
½ small green chilli, deseeded
  and diced

For the Pickling Liquid

300 ml (10 fl oz/
  1¼ cups) water
150 ml (5 fl oz/scant ⅔ cup)
  white wine vinegar
15 g (½ oz) salt (ideally without
  an anti-caking agent)
1 teaspoon peppercorns and/
  or juniper berries
3 bay leaves

Oțet cu Ierburi

HERBY VINEGAR

A super easy recipe for infused vinegar, which can be used in salads or marinades. Use any type of herbs, garlic, chilli peppers or dried seeds to make the recipe your own.

Makes 1 x 350 ml (12 fl oz) bottle

3 rosemary sprigs
3 summer savory sprigs
4–5 thyme sprigs
320 ml (11¼ fl oz/1⅓ cups) cider vinegar

First, sterilise the bottle by submerging it in a saucepan of water lined with a cloth. Bring the water to around 80°C (175°F) and keep it at this temperature for 15 minutes.

Meanwhile, warm the vinegar but do not boil it.

Remove the sterilised bottle from the pan, add all the herbs and pour the vinegar over. Seal and allow to cool, then transfer to the refrigerator. It will be ready after 3–4 days, and keeps improving over time. Use within 3 months.

Dulceata de Morcovi

CARROT JAM

An elegant jam made from a very humble vegetable, the carrot. It has a wonderful colour and is traditionally served with a glass of cold water and some Turkish coffee.

Makes 3 x 250 g (9 oz) jars

400 g (14 oz) carrots, grated
350 ml (12 fl oz/scant
    1½ cups) water
zest and juice of 1 large orange
200 g (7 oz/scant 1 cup) jam sugar with pectin

Put the carrots with the measured water in a large pan and bring to a simmer. Cook over a medium heat for 10 minutes until the carrots start to soften. Add the orange zest and juice, then the sugar, and cook over a low heat for 30 minutes, stirring from time to time. The juice needs to be slightly thick before you turn the heat off, and the jam will thicken further as it cools down. The result will be similar to runny honey and not a well-set jam.

Meanwhile, sterilise your jars (see page 247). When the jam is ready, remove the jars from the water, carefully pour in the hot jam right up to the brim and seal. Return the filled jars to the pan, bring back to 80°C (175°F) and simmer for 10 minutes. Leave to cool in the water, or until they are safe to remove from the pan.

Cafea cu Rom

MARGHILOMAN COFFEE

Marghiloman was a respected Romanian politician in the early 20th century, and well-known for his love of coffee. One day, while he was out hunting, his butler forgot to bring water to prepare it and, thinking on his feet, replaced it with rum. This is more or less what we are going to do in the recipe below. Marghiloman coffee became a fashion frenzy in the capital, Bucharest, and a mark of sophistication and good taste for anyone who ordered it.

Makes 4 small cups

300 ml (10 fl oz/1 ¼ cups) water
1 teaspoon light brown sugar
30 g (1 oz/6 tablespoons) Arabica coffee
30 ml (2 tablespoons) dark rum

In a small coffee pot, warm the water with the sugar, stirring to dissolve the sugar well. Don't bring it to the boil, it just needs to be slightly warm. Add the coffee and rum, turn the heat to medium and wait for it to heat up and swell to the rim. Take it off the heat immediately, so the swell calms down, then repeat one more time. Keep a close eye on it, as it can burst over very quickly. Set aside for 2–3 minutes, then divide between 4 small coffee cups.

Gutuiată

QUINCE APERITIF

It is a Romanian tradition to make drinks at home, from wine to brandies and liqueurs. Here is a version with quince, delicately perfumed and made when quince is in season.

Makes around 500 ml (17 fl oz/2 cups)

500 g (1 lb 2 oz) quince, unpeeled and sliced
300 ml (10 fl oz/1 ¼ cups)
    dark rum
200 ml (7 fl oz/scant 1
    cup) vodka
50 g (2 oz/¼ cup) caster (superfine) sugar
2 vanilla pods (beans), split

Combine all the ingredients in a jar in which the quince slices can fit snugly, ensuring the quince stays submerged in the liquid. Refrigerate for 10 weeks, shaking the jar every now and then to dissolve the sugar.

After 10 weeks, strain the liqueur through a sieve (fine-mesh strainer) into sterilised bottles (see page 247) and enjoy over the following months.

Must

FERMENTED GRAPE JUICE

Must is a very young wine, only a few days old, usually made right at the start of the wine-making season. In Romania, many people have grapevines in their gardens and make wine at home, so the season for *must* is incredibly short but delectable. They usually put aside a small quantity of juice from the large batch destined to make wine, add a little sugar and allow it to ferment to make a lightly fizzy drink that even kids can enjoy. Today, you can find it sold in bottles in stores, like any other product that transcends seasons. It is pronounced 'moost' like the 'oo' in the word 'room'.

Makes 850 ml (28 fl oz/generous 3¼ cups)

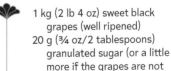

1 kg (2 lb 4 oz) sweet black grapes (well ripened)
20 g (¾ oz/2 tablespoons) granulated sugar (or a little more if the grapes are not super sweet)

Crush the grapes in an electric juice maker or food processor to extract the juice. Depending on the grapes, you may need to add a splash of water to thin the juice a little. Put them through a sieve (fine-mesh strainer) set over a bowl and press down with the back of a spoon to extract as much liquid as possible. Discard the leftover skins.

Add the sugar to the juice to kick start the fermentation. Pour everything into a sterilised bottle, seal it and place in a warm room for 2–3 days, shaking the bottle from time to time to dissolve the sugar. Open the bottle every day to allow the gases to escape.

After this time, taste it and decide if it's ready or whether you need to ferment it for longer. It only needs to be lightly fizzy. If it is ready, refrigerate for 24 hours before drinking.

Drink in small quantities because it is an effective (sometimes instant) diuretic. It will keep fermenting in the refrigerator, so open the bottle carefully. It gets better over the following few days, so my advice is to experiment and see how it matures and how you like it at different stages.

Braga

FERMENTED MILLET DRINK

In Romania, *braga* has been a summer drink for centuries. Made popular by the Ottoman armies, it has remained in our repertoire ever since, even if today we see fewer vendors. Making *braga* the traditional way had a few stages. Initially, the millet was cooked in water until soft, allowed to ferment, then shaped into patties and dried outdoors in the heat of the sun (or in the oven). This stage made it portable and storable. The patties were then added to water with sugar or honey, some lemon juice or verjus, and allowed to ferment together. Strained and chilled, the juice was then sold by street vendors or mobile sellers.

The recipe below is shorter since we no longer need portable millet tablets to make this drink in the summer.

Makes 1.2 litres (40 fl oz/5 cups)

100 g (3½ oz/⅔ cup) millet
2 litres (68 fl oz/8½ cups) water
120 g (½ 4 oz/generous ½ cup) caster (superfine) sugar
juice of 1 small lemon

In a large pan, boil the millet in the measured water until very soft. Turn off the heat, add the sugar and stir well to dissolve it. Allow to cool, then add the lemon juice and transfer it to a clean, sterilised jar and seal. Place the jar in a warm room and allow the millet to ferment for 2–5 days, stirring it every day.

When you see the mixture form bubbles around the top, you can taste it. It needs to be slightly acidic. Strain it through a sieve (fine-mesh strainer) into a bottle and refrigerate.

Served chilled and within a couple of days.

Index

L

lamb
  fried lamb pastries with watermelon **67**
  lamb and spring onion stew with flatbreads **203**
  lamb soup with pearl barley and mint **128—9**
  pastrami lamb chops with polenta **208**
Lancashire cheese
  vitamin soup with spring onions, lettuce and eggs **118**
lardons
  Haiduc stew **207**
leeks
  Black Sea orzo and toasted vermicelli pilaf with haddock **186**
  eggs with sautéed leeks and courgettes **35**
  lamb soup with pearl barley and mint **128—9**
  leek and rice pie **68**
  leek stew with olives **145**
lentil and burghul wheat stuffed peppers **158**
lettuce
  crème fraîche cucumber and lettuce salad **111**
  pot-roasted chicken with braised broad beans, lettuce and wild chicory **200**
  vitamin soup with spring onions, lettuce and eggs **118**
love breads **80**

M

mackerel
  smoked mackerel salad **39**
Marghiloman coffee **254**
milk
  millet porridge with milk and jam **38**
  savoury bread and butter pudding with bacon **33**
  semolina milk soufflé **218**
millet
  fermented millet drink **260**
  millet and mushroom stuffed vine leaves **161**
  millet porridge with milk and jam **38**
mint
  garden pea spread with mint **95**
  lamb soup with pearl barley and mint **128—9**
  soup with fish dumplings and mint **125**
mushrooms
  millet and mushroom stuffed vine leaves **161**
  mushroom and spring onion loaf **104**
  mushrooms in sour cream sauce with polenta **140**
Must **259**

N

noodles
  Tatar soup with beans and wide noodles **126**
  wide noodles with sauerkraut **155**

O

olives
  leek stew with olives **145**
  potato and egg salad with olives **88**
Oltenian ash bread **58**
Oltenian roasted chard with garlic dressing and creamy polenta **100**
Oltenian wine and cornmeal crackers **76**
onions
  bean stew with cheese flatbreads and pickled onions **142**
  boiled eggs with sour cream sauce and paprika onions **45**
  filo pastries with onions and walnuts **77**
  fried salmon morsels with paprika onion salad and potato wedges **170**

P

pan-fried sea bream with garlic sauce and polenta **175**
pancakes
  Eibenthal potato pancakes with horseradish cream and gherkins **42**
  St. Helena yeasted pancakes with poppy seeds **30**
parsnip
  lamb soup with pearl barley and mint **128—9**
  Oltenian stuffed dried pepper soup **116—17**
pasta
  Black Sea orzo and toasted vermicelli pilaf with haddock **186**
  wide noodles with sauerkraut **155**
pastrami lamb chops with polenta **208**
pearl barley
  lamb soup with pearl barley and mint **128—9**
peas
  garden pea and broad bean stew with eggy bread **152**
  garden pea spread with mint **95**
peppers
  fish and roasted vegetable spread **108—9**
  fish paprikash with egg dumplings **178**
  lamb soup with pearl barley and mint **128—9**
  lentil and burghul wheat stuffed peppers **158**

Q

R

S

Acknowledgements

I owe a big thank you to Lina and Radmila Dragotoiu, mother and daughter, who were the best ambassadors of the Serbian communities in Romania. If you travel to Sviniţa, stop at Lina's place and buy her delicious fig jam and brandy.

While you are in the area, visit the neighbouring Czech villages, and use Banat.cz to find accommodation.

A huge thank you to George Dumitru and Daniel Popa from Ţesturi Pâine for welcoming us with open arms, they sell the traditional bread making oven online.

Thank you to Pierre Bortowski from Cula Curtişoara, for his time and patient explanations. In Dobrogea, thank you to Bianca Folescu for her hospitality in her traditional guest house. If you visit, look for Suvenir de Dobrogea online and send Bianca an email, you can't be in better hands. In the neighbouring village, Jurilovca, I owe Mrs Evghenia Turcu from the Lipoveni community a thank you for her time and knowledge.

A huge thank you to Filiz Ismail, the President of the Turkish Women Association of UDTTMR, and to her husband Ecrem, for their help driving me around traditional villages and for all the information and documents they put at my disposal. Through Filiz, I met the amazing Mrs Enise Ali, who runs Jade, a traditional and beautifully decorated Tatar restaurant in Constanţa.

Thank you to Mrs Ulcher Memet in Babadag town for the best pickled aubergines I've ever had.

For a good guide in Constanţa, look for Diana Slav.

Thank you to the generous Petya Borisova for sharing her family story with me, then to the Union of Bulgarians in Romania and to Petăr Velciov from the Pauliceni Catholic Bulgarian communities in Banat for talking me through the history of Bulgarians here.

Thank you to Librăriile Cărturești and Humanitas and to GastroArt Publishing and Cosmin Dragomir for stocking and producing important books about Romanian culture and cuisine.

Thank you to the Romanian Ministry of Agriculture for the information about Dobrogeană pie and to the Museum of Galaţi for sending the details about the historic King Caroll chocolate biscuits.

Thank you to so many others, whom I mentioned in this book in the recipes or chapter introductions.

To deepen your knowledge about this part of the world and its ethnic groups, you can read Marie Favereau *The Horde*, Alan W. Fisher *The Crimean Tatars*, Wim Van Meurs and Alina Mungiu-Pippidi *Ottomans into Europeans*, Dr Özge Samancı *La cuisine d'Istanbul au XIXe siècle*, Mark Mazower *The Balkans*, Judith Herrin *Byzantium*, Nick Thorpe *Danube*, Claudio Magris *Danube*, Neal Ascherson *Black Sea* and Cosmin Dragomir *Curatorul de Zacuscă* and many others.

Published in 2024 by Hardie Grant Books

Hardie Grant Books (London)
5th & 6th Floors
52–54 Southwark Street
London SE1 1UN

hardiegrantbooks.com

British Library Cataloguing-in-Publication
Data. A catalogue record for this book
is available from the British Library.

Danube
ISBN: 9781784887049

10 9 8 7 6 5 4 3 2 1

Publishing Director: Kajal Mistry
Senior Commissioning Editor: Kate Burkett
Project Editor: Emily Preece-Morrison
Cover Design & Illustrations: Evi-O.Studio | Eloise Myatt
Internal Design & Illustrations: Evi-O.Studio | Susan Le
Typesetting: Evi-O.Studio | Doreen Zheng
Photography: Issy Croker
Food stylist: Joss Herd
Food stylist's assistant: Hattie Arnold
Prop stylist: Kitty Coles
Copy Editor: Emily Preece-Morrison
Proofreader: Sarah Prior
Indexer: Cathy Heath
Senior Production Controller: Sabeena Atchia

Colour Reproduction by p2d
Printed and bound in China by C&C Offset Printing Co., Ltd.